# APPLE®
# INTERFACING

by

**Jonathan A. Titus, David G. Larsen, and
Christopher A. Titus**

Howard W. Sams & Co., Inc.
4300 WEST 62ND ST. INDIANAPOLIS, INDIANA 46268 USA

**FIRST EDITION**
**FIRST PRINTING—1981**

International Standard Book Number: 0-672-21862-3
Library of Congress Catalog Card Number: 81-84282

Edited by: *Bob Manville*
Illustrated by: *Jill E. Martin*

*Printed in the United States of America.*

# Preface

The purpose in writing this book is to introduce you to the signals within the Apple®* II computer and to show you how these signals can be used to control external devices under the control of BASIC-language programs. A general-purpose computer interface breadboard has been developed to speed your circuit design and testing so that you can easily perform the many interesting experiments that are included in the book. By using a design system such as the one described in this book, you will spend your time concentrating on the principles involved, rather than troubleshooting your circuits. However, you will have the opportunity to build and test many digital circuits, as well as circuits that use digital-to-analog and analog-to-digital converters.

We have chosen to use the Apple II computer with 16K of read/write memory, and the Applesoft™† BASIC interpreter program. This software provides a great deal of flexibility and it is worth having it available when you are using external interface circuits. The Applesoft BASIC interpreter has two general-purpose commands that can be used to transfer information to and from the computer. These instructions are easily mastered, without requiring a detailed understanding of the 6502 microprocessor integrated circuit (IC) that is used as the "heart" of the Apple.

First we will introduce you to the control signals that are available from the Apple computer for interfacing, and we will show you how they are used. Some of the signals will not be described, since they are generally not used in interface circuits, and are meant to be used by special interface devices that are manufactured commercially.

Our next step is to show you how the Apple can identify or address external devices through the use of two general-purpose instructions, PEEK and POKE. These commands are central to the control of external devices; we spend some time covering their operation and the use of a variety of circuits that can be used to identify specific input/output, or I/O devices. You will also see how the Apple can transfer information to and from external devices over the bidirectional data

---

*Apple and Apple II are registered trademarks of Apple Computer, Inc.
†Applesoft is a trademark of Apple Computer, Inc.

bus; the basic circuits used for *input ports* and *output ports* are described in detail. Real circuits are provided, so that you can quickly use the many examples in designing your own interface devices.

You will also see the power of BASIC-language programs—as the data is processed within the computer to provide meaningful results. Simple control programs are provided to show you how BASIC-language programs and I/O devices can interact. You will be able to write simple control and data processing programs to go along with your I/O ports and devices.

Since the computer is not always synchronized to external devices, there must be some interaction between the computer and the various I/O devices so that each knows when the other is ready for some appropriate action. This leads us to the topic of flags—those signals that are used by the computer and by external I/O devices to allow information to be transferred in an orderly fashion. Since flags are important, we spend some time on them and on the corresponding circuits that are actually used in external devices. Software is covered too, since the flag circuits are useless unless they can be sensed by a control program.

We have assumed that you have a fairly good understanding of the commands in Applesoft BASIC. If you are just getting started with the Apple computer, we hope that you will take some time to review the simple commands, such as FOR, GOTO, IF . . . THEN, PRINT, and INPUT. Other commands will be introduced in the text and experiments, and we will provide the details of their operation. At the end of this book, the use of these and other commands should be second-nature.

In Chapter 6, we have provided 16 detailed, step-by-step experiments that you can perform to reinforce the many interfacing principles that have been developed in the text. You will also see the power of BASIC-language programs for interface control and for actually processing the information that is involved in transfers to and from I/O devices. We have made an effort to cover a broad spectrum of interesting interface applications. Throughout the experiments, you will see that the same basic principles apply to all of the interface circuits, from the simplest to the most complex.

We realize that it is difficult to write a book like this for an audience that has a wide range of backgrounds, from the beginner to the advanced user. Thus, we have chosen to start at some middle point. We have chosen to skip basic binary numbering, decimal-to-binary conversions, basic digital electronics, and breadboarding. These topics are covered in detail in other books, and the reader who is in the middle of our assumed spectrum of readers probably has a good understanding of these topics. In some places, a paragraph or two of review material have been provided, just to serve as a refresher. We make no attempt to provide much detail here, simply enough to get you started.

We have assumed some familiarity with SN7400-family digital integrated circuits, or chips, such as the SN7402 quad NOR gate and the SN7475 quad latch chip. Other complex chips will be introduced and explained in sufficient detail so that you can use them as shown in the text or experiments. If you wish to use these devices in other applications, we suggest that you obtain the necessary data sheets from the manufacturers. The data sheets will provide the necessary information for a wide variety of uses, and they will also reflect any basic changes or modifications that may have been made to an "updated" device, or one that has been "enhanced" with some special feature.

The Apple II computer has eight general-purpose 50-conductor interface connectors in its case. The basic bus signals used in the experiments are derived from the signals at these connectors, so if you decide to design and build some of your own interface circuits that will be plugged into one of these "slots," you will find the same signals are readily available at the edge connectors. However, there are also some special-purpose signals that are generated by the Apple to make the interfacing task somewhat easier. These signals and their uses are described in detail in Chapter 7. Since the signals are not general purpose, but are specific to the Apple, and in many cases, specific to a particular connector, they are described last. To show you how these signals are used, a simple asynchronous-serial communication interface circuit is described, and software to control it is listed. This type of interface can be used to communicate with other computers, serial printers, modems, and other interface devices that use the asynchronous-serial data format.

We have not described assembly-language programming, since this is a specialized topic and requires a great deal of background. However, we have provided one simple assembly-language subroutine for you to use in several of the experiments. There is a good reason for including this subroutine; the equivalent function is not readily available in Applesoft. The function required is the logical ANDing of 8-bit bytes. The logical AND in Applesoft is simply a true-or-false AND operation, and it cannot be easily used for bit ANDing. The assembly-language subroutine also provides you with an introduction to how such routines can be accessed by a BASIC-language program. We have chosen to use the more complicated USR(X) command, rather than the CALL command, since we think that more will be learned.

We found that there were some limitations to the Apple. For example, there is no simple "rounding" command that can be used to round a number to a specific number of decimal digits, for example

4.1986 to 4.20. Likewise, the absence of a bit-by-bit ANDing command was a limitation that was overcome with an assembly-language routine. We also found that the potentially useful WAIT command that is used to test individual bits will "hang up" the computer if the condition is not found. The computer continues to wait if the condition is not met, and you must reset the computer to get your program going again. A color display and nice graphics are available, although we used a black/white monitor in our system.

Most of the special purpose chips, such as the analog converters, have been chosen because of their simplicity, low cost, and availability. This is not meant to be an endorsement of these products. As your interfacing sophistication increases, you will find other special-purpose devices that can serve the same function, but perhaps with added features, more resolution, different power supplies, etc. Our aim is to get you started, and not to provide you with a sourcebook of every possible interface to the Apple computer system. An impossible task in any case.

If you are interested in some additional reading about more advanced topics, we recommend:

*6502 Software Design* (21656).
*Programming & Interfacing the 6502, With Experiments* (21651).
*Microcomputer-Analog Converter Software and Hardware Interfacing* (21540).

We also recommend *TRS-80 Interfacing, Book 2*. While written around the TRS-80 computer, this book details more advanced interfacing topics such as driving high-current/high-voltage loads, serial communications, remote control, analog converters, filtering and data processing, and other interesting topics. You will quickly see that the similarities between the TRS-80 and Apple are much greater than their differences. Control signals and BASIC commands are almost identical. All of the books noted above are available from Howard W. Sams & Co., Inc., 4300 West 62nd Street, Indianapolis, IN 46268.

The pin configuration figures used in most of the figures, unless otherwise noted, are provided through the courtesy of Texas Instruments, Incorporated. The names Apple and Applesoft are trademarks of Apple Computer, Inc., Cupertino, CA. The name TRS-80 is a registered trademark of Radio Shack.

We hope that you enjoy this book, and that it leads you to design and build some interface circuits of your own.

JONATHAN A. TITUS, CHRISTOPHER A. TITUS and DAVID G. LARSEN
*"The Blacksburg Group"*

# Contents

# CHAPTER 6

# CHAPTER 7

# APPENDIX A

# APPENDIX B

# APPENDIX C

# APPENDIX D

# APPENDIX E

# CHAPTER 1

# 6502 Processor

The Apple II® (Apple®) computer system by Apple Computer, Inc., uses the 6502-type of microprocessor integrated circuit. This "chip" forms the heart of the central processing unit (CPU) of the computer, the place where the actual mathematical, logical, decision-making, and other operations take place. The 6502-type microprocessor chip is manufactured by MOS Technology (Norristown, PA 19401), Rockwell International (Anaheim, CA 92803) and Synertek Corporation (Santa Clara, CA 95051).

The 6502 is an 8-bit processor. Thus, all of the mathematical, logical, data transfer, input and output operations operate on eight binary bits at a time. Each bit, of course, can be either a logic one or a logic zero. The 6502 uses an 8-bit data bus to transfer information between itself and various memory locations and input/output (I/O) devices such as a keyboard, printer, etc. In cases where the value of the information exceeds the limit of eight bits, multiples of 8-bit data words are used. Each 8-bit data word is generally referred to as a *byte*.

You should realize that the maximum value that can be expressed with eight bits is $11111111_2$ or $255_{10}$. If larger values are to be operated on in an 8-bit computer system, then multibyte operations are required. Generally, this means that corresponding data bytes in two data words are operated on, followed by the operation being performed on the next corresponding set of bytes in the large data words. In this way large values, beyond the value of 255, may be readily processed. It is important to remember, though, that the

---

Apple and Apple II are registered trademarks of Apple Computer, Inc.

Apple CPU can only process and transfer eight bits or one byte at a time.

The 6502 uses a single set of eight pins to make the connection with the data bus in the computer. This data bus is used to transfer information both to and from the computer. This type of a bus is called *bidirectional,* since it allows information to flow in two different directions. This is much like a highway that is used to allow vehicles to drive one way in the morning and to allow vehicles to travel in the opposite direction in the evening.

The 6502 generates control signals on the integrated circuit that are used both internally and externally to supervise and manage the flow of information on the bus, in one direction at a time. We will explore the generation and use of these signals later in this book.

### MEMORY

All computer systems have some memory associated with them. In general, the memory is used to store both a program that will control the operation of the computer, as well as the information that is to be processed. In the 6502 computer, each memory location can be used to store eight bits of information, or one byte of data. Most memories consist of multiples of these one-byte storage locations, generally in multiples of 1024, abbreviated 1K.

The memory locations must be addressed in some way so that the computer knows exactly where it is to store data or obtain program step information. The 6502 microprocessor chip has 16 address outputs allowing it to specify any one of $2^{16}$ or 65,536 memory locations, each of which can contain one byte. This is often shortened to 64K, indicating that 64K *bytes* of information can be addressed. In almost all microcomputer memory systems, each memory location is uniquely addressed with a 16-bit address.

The address bus lines are labeled A0 through A15, corresponding to the least-significant bit (LSB) through the most-significant bit (MSB), respectively. The LSB and MSB can both be either a logic one or a logic zero, but their *position* gives the LSB a *value* of zero or one and the MSB a *value* of zero or 32,768. Since the 6502 is an 8-bit processor, the address lines are frequently split into two groups of eight lines each, A7-A0 and A15-A8. The lines A7-A0 are referred to as the low or LO address, while lines A15-A8 are referred to as the high or HI address. In many 6502-based computers, the HI address is also called the *page address,* since the memory may be arbitrarily divided into 256 pages, with 256 bytes per page. The uses of the address bus will be explored further when software instructions are discussed and when interface circuits are developed. Unlike the data bus, the address bus is unidirectional, the address information flows

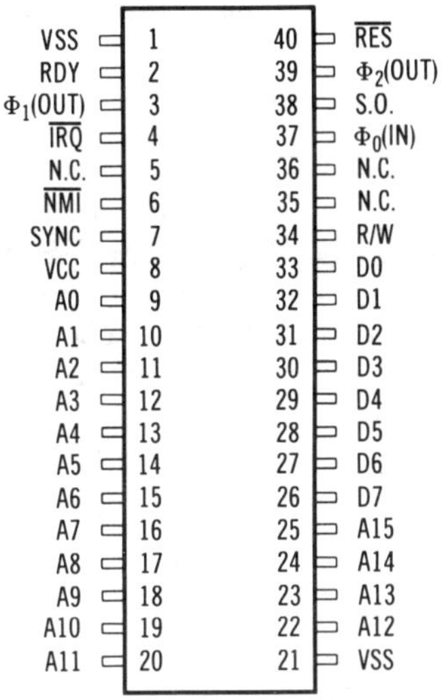

```
VSS    ⊏  1       40 ⊐  RES
RDY    ⊏  2       39 ⊐  Φ₂(OUT)
Φ₁(OUT) ⊏  3       38 ⊐  S.0.
IRQ    ⊏  4       37 ⊐  Φ₀(IN)
N.C.   ⊏  5       36 ⊐  N.C.
NMI    ⊏  6       35 ⊐  N.C.
SYNC   ⊏  7       34 ⊐  R/W
VCC    ⊏  8       33 ⊐  D0
A0     ⊏  9       32 ⊐  D1
A1     ⊏ 10       31 ⊐  D2
A2     ⊏ 11       30 ⊐  D3
A3     ⊏ 12       29 ⊐  D4
A4     ⊏ 13       28 ⊐  D5
A5     ⊏ 14       27 ⊐  D6
A6     ⊏ 15       26 ⊐  D7
A7     ⊏ 16       25 ⊐  A15
A8     ⊏ 17       24 ⊐  A14
A9     ⊏ 18       23 ⊐  A13
A10    ⊏ 19       22 ⊐  A12
A11    ⊏ 20       21 ⊐  VSS
```

Fig. 1-1. 6502 Microprocessor chip pin configuration.

in only one direction, from the CPU to the memory and to external devices.

The pin configuration of the 6502 is shown in Fig. 1-1. Although most of the other signals may be meaningless to you now, you should be able to identify the 8 data bus input/output pins and the 16 address output pins.

Since the memory section is being discussed, there are two basic types of memory devices used in microcomputer systems. They are:

1. *Read/Write*—Read/Write (R/W) memory is used for the storage of data that will be changed or updated. The computer must be able to place the information in a memory location and then be able to read it back. Programs that will change are also stored in R/W memory for the same reason. The lowest cost Apple computer contains 16,384 or 16K bytes of R/W memory.
2. *Read-Only*—Read-only memory (ROM) is used when data values and program steps will not be altered. The BASIC interpreter program in your Apple system is contained in read-only memory chips. The Apple BASIC interpreter is stored in 12K of ROM.

There are various sub-classes of these types of memory devices. The R/W memories may be either *static* or *dynamic*. Static memory chips will maintain the values stored in them until they are changed. Dynamic memories require refreshing by external hardware every few milliseconds or they will "forget" or lose the data stored in them. The R/W memories in the Apple are dynamic, with the necessary refreshing circuitry contained on the computer printed-circuit board.

There are many types of read-only memories. The various types are generally all static, the differences occurring in the means of storing the 8-bit values in the memory locations. The two most important types are *mask-programmed* and *field-programmed*. The mask-programmed devices have data values, program steps, etc., stored in them during the various manufacturing steps. They are generally referred to as ROMs. The field-programmable devices require some kind of special programming circuitry to store the logic ones and zeros in the various locations. Some of the field programmable ROMs, or PROMs, as they are generally called, can be erased under high-intensity ultraviolet light. They can then be reprogrammed. This is very useful when programs are being developed that will be stored in read-only memory. It does not require the development of masks and chips—an expensive process—each time a program bug is found or a change is made.

A few final words are required about semiconductor memory devices. The read-write devices are *volatile*, since data (your program and values) will "evaporate" or disappear when power is removed from the system. The read-only memories, on the other hand, are considered to be nonvolatile, since they will maintain the data or program steps (the BASIC interpreter) when the power has been removed.

Most memory integrated-circuit packages or chips do not have all 16 of the address lines connected to them. They have only enough address connections to uniquely address the memory locations within the individual chip. Thus, a 64-byte chip, small by standards of today, would only have 6 address line inputs while a 1024 (1K) byte memory chip would have 10 address line inputs. Memory chips such as these have an additional control or chip-enable input that allows banks or groups of the chips to be selected, one set at a time. Various decoding and selecting circuits may be used, thus allowing a 32K block of memory to be constructed from 64-byte or 1K byte chips, or even combinations of the two. The main point here is that the memory chips do not require all 16 address lines *to be connected directly to them,* although some combination of all 16 address bits will be used to uniquely select one byte. You should not be confused when you are confronted with a 1K × 4 bit memory that only has 10 address inputs and a chip enable input. This concept will be developed further as you study input/output data transfers.

One control signal is generated by the 6502 processor chip to control the flow of information on the data bus. This signal is noted as READ/$\overline{\text{WRITE}}$, or more simply, R/$\overline{\text{W}}$. Whenever a read, or a write, operation is to take place, the 6502 must specify a 16-bit address to locate the memory "cell" that is to be involved in the transfer. In this case, the cell is an 8-bit word or byte.

The "bar" over part of the signal notation indicates that when the signal is a logic zero, a write operation is taking place; and when in the logic one state, a read operation is taking place. Thus, a single line controls all of the memory functions. In some 6502-based computer systems and peripherals, you may see the signal "split," to provide two memory control signals, memory read ($\overline{\text{MEMR}}$ or $\overline{\text{MR}}$), and memory write ($\overline{\text{MEMW}}$ or $\overline{\text{MW}}$). This takes some additional gating, so in most cases, the R/$\overline{\text{W}}$ signal is used by itself. It is available at pin 34 on the 6502 microprocessor chip.

You may also see the notation RAM used to incorrectly signify read/write memory. The acronym RAM stands for *random-access memory*. In fact, all of the modern, easy-to-use memory devices are random access, since one may address one location and then any other, without having to sequence through all of the locations between the two addresses.

Pin configurations for typical memory chips have been provided in Fig. 1-2.

For additional information about memory devices, we refer you to

- *Intel Memory Design Handbook,* Intel Corporation, Santa Clara, CA 95051, 1975.

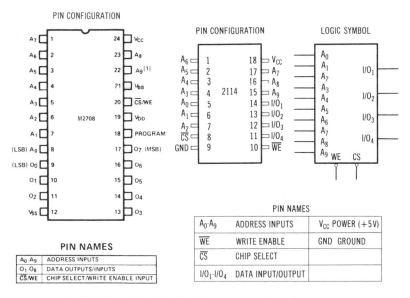

Fig. 1-2. Pin configuration for 2708 1K × 8 PROM and 2114 1K × 4 R/W memory.

- *The 8080A/9080A MOS Microprocessor Handbook,* Advanced Micro Devices, Inc., Sunnyvale, CA 94086, 1977.
- *Mostek Memory Products Catalog,* Mostek Corporation, Carrollton, TX 75006, 1977.
- *Bipolar and CMOS Memory Data Book,* Harris Semiconductor Prod. Div., Melbourne, FL 32901, 1978.

## INPUT/OUTPUT (I/O) DEVICES

Most microcomputer-based systems are worthless without some attached I/O devices. These devices may be standard peripherals, such as card readers, printers, displays, or they may be sensors, controllers, and other devices that most people do not normally associate with computers. The Apple is no exception. It already has several I/O devices associated with it: a television display, a cassette recorder, and a keyboard.

Other I/O devices can be added to your computer. These devices may be of your own design or they may be standard, commercially available devices that are compatible with the Apple. These I/O devices are much like the individual memory locations that were discussed in the previous section. The I/O devices are attached to the data bus, since data is transferred to them and from them, and they are also connected to the address bus so that they may be uniquely addressed by the 6502 microprocessor chip.

A control signal, READ/$\overline{\text{WRITE}}$ or R/$\overline{\text{W}}$, is used to synchronize the flow of data to and from the I/O devices. This signal is also used in 6502-based computer systems to control the flow of information to and from the memory chips. Thus, there is no differentiation between memory addresses and I/O device addresses in 6502-based computers. In computers that are based upon the 8085- or Z-80-type microprocessor chips, there are different techniques that are used to address memory and I/O devices independently. Since only one synchronizing signal is used to control memory and I/O devices, the Apple's 6502 processor will be either reading or writing at all times. When the R/$\overline{\text{W}}$ signal is a logic one, the 6502 is reading information *from* the data bus. When the R/$\overline{\text{W}}$ signal is a logic zero, the 6502 is writing data *to* an external I/O device, or *to* a memory location. The "bar" over the W simply means that the write operation takes place when the R/$\overline{\text{W}}$ signal is a logic zero. You may see other signals with such bars over their names. This simply means that the signals are active in the logic zero state.

Since we will be concentrating on the use of I/O devices with the Apple, we have left a great deal of the specific discussion to the remaining sections.

## Review

At this point, you should understand that the 6502 transfers and operates on eight bits of data at a time. Complex calculations and operations often require multiple groups of eight bits or bytes. The bytes are transferred to and from the 6502 CPU on an 8-bit bus.

**Table 1-1. Control Signals Used for Interfacing**

| DATA BUS | D7-D0 | An 8-bit bidirectional set of lines for transfer of information between the CPU and I/O devices. |
|---|---|---|
| ADDRESS BUS | A15-A0 | A 16-bit unidirectional address bus used to address both memory and I/O devices. |
| | A15-A8 | HI address bus, most-significant eight address bits. |
| | A7-A0 | LO address bus, least-significant eight address bits. |
| CONTROL SIGNAL | R/$\overline{W}$ | Read/write control signal. |

NOTES: The "bar" notation, i.e., $\overline{W}$, indicates a logic zero is the "active" state, the state that causes the corresponding action to take place.

In each case in which a signal is enumerated, the numbers increase as the significance of the bits increases, i.e., A15 = most-significant address bit (MSB).

The 6502 uses a 16-bit address bus to address individual memory location and I/O devices. The address bus is frequently broken into a HI and LO address bus, of eight bits each. The single control signal, R/$\overline{W}$, controls the flow of information to and from the 6502 CPU. The signals and their designations are noted in Table 1-1.

## SOFTWARE I/O CONTROL INSTRUCTIONS

### I/O Commands

The Apple computer has a number of instructions that are used to control I/O devices. For the most part, though, these instructions are used to control specific I/O devices or to perform specific functions. Without realizing it, you are already familiar with some, if not all, of these I/O instructions.

Here are some specific examples of these I/O control instructions, to refresh your memory.

The INPUT and PRINT commands are probably familiar to you. The INPUT command causes a BASIC program to stop and wait for an input from the keyboard. The PRINT command causes an answer or string of characters to be "printed" on the tv screen.

**Example 1-1. A Simple I/O Program**

```
10   INPUT "VALUE OF X IS"; X
20   PRINT " INPUT VALUE WAS"; X
```

If you executed the program in Example 1-1, the value associated with the variable, X, would have to be entered into the computer before the program passed control to statement 20. These two types of I/O statements are frequently used to allow an operator to enter a value and to see it displayed. There are many variations of both the INPUT and PRINT commands, but these two examples serve to illustrate the point; you have already been using I/O operations in BASIC-language programs without difficulty.

You may have already discovered that there are also *graphic display* I/O commands in BASIC, too. These are commands such as HOME, PLOT X,Y and SCRN (X,Y). The HOME command clears the screen, and places the blinking cursor at the "home" position in the upper left-hand corner of the tv screen. The PLOT and SCRN commands require the use of "coordinates" to indicate where an operation is to take place.

The program in Example 1-2 shows how some simple graphic display commands are used in a short program. This program generates a display of randomly changing colored dots on the tv screen. If you are using a black-and-white (b/w) tv, you will see the dots in varying shades of gray.

**Example 1-2. A Random Color Pattern Generator Using I/O Commands**

```
10   GR
20   X = INT(40 * RND(1)) + 1
30   Y = INT(40 * RND(1)) + 1
40   COLOR = INT(15 * RND(1)) + 1
50   PLOT X,Y
60   GOTO 20
```

There are two other commands that you may not have considered to be I/O commands. These are the LOAD and SAVE commands that are used to read and store programs on cassette tapes. Each command causes a preset series of operations to take place, controlling the cassette recorder. The use of these commands is fairly obvious, so we will not provide an example.

Other I/O commands are the IN#X and PR#X operations that are associated with special I/O devices that can be substituted for the keyboard and tv display. It is important that you realize that these I/O instructions are specific to the Apple computer and its BASIC-language interpreter program. These instructions would be meaningless to other 6502-based computer systems, unless they used the Apple BASIC program. The instructions are also specific to one I/O device, i.e., the HOME command will not have an effect on the cassette recorder, *or any other I/O device.* Likewise, the INPUT command controls the input of values only from the keyboard on the console.

## General-Purpose I/O Commands

Although there are some general-purpose I/O commands in the INTEGER BASIC interpreter program for the Apple computer, for this book we have chosen to use what we consider to be the more flexible APPLESOFT BASIC interpreter program. If you wish to convert your Apple computer to this program, a local Apple computer dealer can assist you.

The two I/O device commands are PEEK and POKE. They are used to transfer data to an external device from the computer (POKE), and to the computer from an external device (PEEK). There is a specific format for these instructions that must be used if the instructions are to operate properly.

Input and output devices will be referred to as *ports*. Thus, an output device will be an *output port* and an input device will be an *input port*. This is standard nomenclature used throughout the microcomputer industry.

The output instruction, POKE, must specify the *address* of the I/O device that is to be involved in the transfer of data and also the value that is to be transferred to the addressed device. The actual format for the POKE instruction is POKE, $x,y$, where the $x$ value represents the *decimal* address of the output device that is to receive the data value, $y$. The data, $y$, must also be a decimal number. Since the 6502 microprocessor chip can address 65536 memory locations, the address must be within the range of 0 to 65535, inclusive. The data value must be within the range of 0 to 255, inclusive, since the computer uses an 8-bit data bus for all data transfers, and the largest number that can be transferred on such a bus is 255.

The value 215 is sent to output port 12684 in the following statement: POKE 12684,215.

The input instruction, PEEK, is similar to the POKE instruction, except that no data value is incorporated into the command. We are interested in determining the value present at the specific input device, so only the decimal address of the input device is specified; PEEK $(x)$, where $x$ is the decimal address of the input device.

It does little good to input a value without doing something with it, so the input command is always incorporated in a complete statement, rather than being a statement by itself. An example of this is Q=PEEK(34579).

In this case, the variable, Q, is assigned the decimal value that has been input from device 34579. It is important that you remember to enclose the address of the input device in parentheses.

Whenever a PEEK command is used, the value that is input will be between 0 and 255, inclusive. Again, this is due to the limitation of 8-bit transfers.

**Table 1-2. Valid Input (PEEK) and Output (POKE) Command Structures**

| | |
|---|---|
| POKE 45124,98 | L = PEEK (23109) |
| POKE N,120 | L = PEEK (Q) |
| POKE 45124,X | |
| POKE X,M | |

The input and output commands may have variables specified within them, rather than specific values for port addresses, and in the case of the POKE command, data values. Thus, all of the PEEK and POKE commands shown in Table 1-2 are valid. We have assumed, of course, that the values for the variables, N, M, X and Q have been specified somewhere in the program prior to the use of the instructions shown in Table 1-2.

Input and output commands in which the address values exceed 65535 will generate an ILLEGAL QUANTITY ERROR in the Apple computer. An attempt to output a numerical data value that exceeds 255 will also generate an ILLEGAL QUANTITY ERROR.

We have provided some examples that show the use of the POKE and PEEK commands. While the programs shown in Example 1-3 can be executed, they will not do anything useful, since you do not have any external I/O ports connected to your computer, at present.

**Example 1-3. Simple I/O Programs for PEEK and POKE Commands**

```
10  INPUT "OUTPUT PORT # =";P
20  INPUT "VALUE FOR OUTPUT"; V
30  POKE P,V
40  GOTO 10
```

```
10  INPUT "INPUT PORT # = "; M
20  PRINT "VALUE AT PORT ="; PEEK (M)
30  GOTO 10
```

Since 6502-based computers cannot distinguish between memory locations that are used for the temporary storage of programs and data, and those that are being used for I/O ports, the PEEK and POKE instructions are frequently used to examine and alter the contents of various memory locations within the Apple. If you POKE information into read/write memory in an indiscriminate fashion, you may "write over" important parts of your program, or information that has been temporarily stored by the BASIC interpreter. The net effect is a "crash" of the computer system, in which your program and data will be lost or significantly altered. It is probably not a good idea to randomly POKE information into various addresses, until some specific guidelines are provided. Of course, you can use the PEEK command to examine the contents of a memory location whenever you wish, since this command will not alter the contents of an examined memory location. From the previous discussion of memory devices, you should realize that the POKE operation will have no effect on the read-only memory devices in the Apple.

## Memory Maps

At this point it is a good idea to take a look at the "maps" of the memory addresses that are used by the Apple. A complete 64K memory map is shown in Fig. 1-3. For the sake of convenience, the memory addresses are provided in both decimal (base-10) and hexadecimal (base-16) notation. The hexadecimal numbers have a suffix of "H" to distinguish them from the decimal numbers.

The memory space for the Apple computer has been divided into four 16K blocks. Three of the blocks have been assigned for R/W memory, and most Apple computers have the R/W #1 block "filled" with read/write memory chips. The remaining R/W blocks may be used for future expansion of R/W memory, if this is required for particular applications. In most cases, we have found that 16K of R/W memory is sufficient. Add-on memory chip kits are available from many suppliers, and most Apple users can probably add the additional memory chips to their system without much difficulty.

The remaining 16K block of memory has been set aside for both ROM and I/O port addressing. The system ROMs for the Apple, which include the BASIC interpreter and the monitor programs, take up 12K of this space. The remaining 4K space is divided into two 2K spaces for I/O addressing and future expansion of the Apple. The I/O block with addresses C000H to C7FFH, inclusive, is the one of major importance for interfacing, since it has been specifically set aside for this purpose and it will never be used in Apple computer systems for any other purpose. Some of the addresses within this 2K block have been used by the Apple for controlling things such as the speaker, the keyboard, and the cassette recorder. The actual address

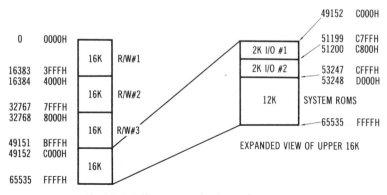

Fig. 1-3. 64K Memory map for the Apple computer.

assignments are shown in Table 1-3. We refer you to *Basic Programming Reference Manual,* and *Apple II Reference Manual,* for details on the actual use of these I/O addresses. These manuals are provided with the Apple II computer, and are also available from Apple Computer, Inc., 10260 Bandley Dr., Cupertino, CA 95014.

The remaining 2K block of memory, C800H-CFFFH, has been set aside for future expansion. You may use this space for additional read-only memory, if you have long programs that you wish to have readily available.

**Table 1-3. Apple I/O Addresses and Their Uses**

| Function | Address | |
|---|---|---|
| | Decimal* | Hexadecimal |
| Keyboard data | 49152 | C000 |
| Clear-keyboard strobe | 49168 | C010 |
| Speaker | 49200 | C030 |
| Cassette Output | 49184 | C020 |
| Cassette Input | 49256 | C060 |
| Flag Inputs | 49249–49251 | C061–C063 |
| Analog Inputs | 49252–49255 | C064–C067 |
| Analog Clear | 49264 | C070 |
| Utility Strobe | 49216 | C040 |

*Only positive addresses given. To calculate negative addresses, just add —65536 to the decimal addresses provided.

In later sections of this book, the actual use of the I/O addresses will be described in detail. At this point, it is sufficient that you understand that a specific set of memory addresses has been set aside for your particular applications. You should also realize that the memory map shown in Fig. 1-3 is particular to the Apple computer. Other 6502-based computers will probably have different memory maps, with R/W memory, read-only memory, and I/O device addresses located in different areas of the map.

## Software Commands and Interface Circuits

As you are probably aware by now, the PEEK and POKE instructions each cause some actions to take place, either at I/O devices or at memory locations, as a direct result of the use of the instruction. Instructions such as A=1.359 will cause some values to be stored in memory, but we do not know what memory locations the Apple has assigned to the variable "A" and we do not know how the value 1.359 has been stored. The PEEK and POKE instructions each cause a definite, known sequence of operations to take place, transferring data bytes, generating control signals, and transferring address information on the address-bus lines. These definite and reproducible actions allow us to use these commands to control I/O devices. We will now explore the actions that each of these software commands causes to take place.

The PEEK and POKE instructions operate in a very similar manner. In each, an address is specified, requiring 16 bits of information. During the execution of either instruction, the *address* information contained within the command is transferred to external devices on the address-bus lines, A15-A0. In this way, the I/O device address is available to all of the devices and circuits that are connected to these address lines, both memory and I/O devices.

When a POKE instruction is used in a program, the data value is also output by the 6502 chip, but on the data-bus lines, D7-D0. Once the data bits and the address bits are "stable" or present on their respective buses in useable form, the 6502 asserts the READ/$\overline{\text{WRITE}}$ signal on the control bus. This synchronizes the acquisition of the data by the I/O device that was addressed. Of course, external circuitry is required to "capture" the data, as well as to identify the selected I/O device and synchronize it with the 6502-based system. A timing diagram for these signals, as they appear on the 6502 system, in this case the Apple, is shown in Fig. 1-4. Of course, the POKE command involves many assembly-language instructions, and the timing diagram shows what happens only during the time of the actual data transfer. At this point, we are only concerned with what the 6502 does during a POKE operation.

When a PEEK instruction is executed, the data is not contained in the instruction, but is acquired from an external I/O device. Only the address is specified. The 16-bit address is placed on the address-

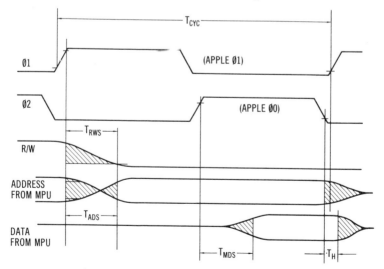

Fig. 1-4. Write operation signal relationships. (See Appendix C.)

bus lines when the PEEK instruction is executed. When the address information is present, the corresponding I/O device must place its data on the data bus so that it may be accepted by the 6502 processor. During a read operation, the R/$\overline{W}$ signal from the 6502 is a logic one. Additional circuitry is required here, too, to select the I/O device and to gate its data onto the data bus. A typical timing diagram for the PEEK command is shown in Fig. 1-5.

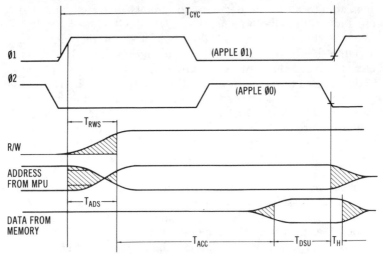

Fig. 1-5. Read operation signal relationships. (See Appendix C.)

We will describe shortly some of the circuits that are used for input and output ports. You have probably realized that while we have described an *I/O port* as one that can either receive data that is output by the microcomputer or transmit data that is input by the microcomputer, some *I/O devices* may actually contain a number of individual I/O ports. Industrial controllers, data storage devices (disks, cassettes), analog converters, and other I/O devices may have a number of I/O ports, since they may require more than eight bits of information from the computer and they may also need to transfer more than eight bits of information to the computer. In any case, transfers of data that contain more than eight bits always involve the transfer of multiple bytes to and from the computer and the individual 8-bit I/O ports. This is important to remember: *information is always transferred eight bits at a time.*

### Software Command—Data Transfer and Control

In most cases, the PEEK and POKE commands will be used to transfer 8-bit data values between the I/O devices or memory locations and the 6502 computer. As we noted previously, some data transfers will require more than eight bits of information, so multiple bytes are transferred, one byte at a time.

There are also cases in which the actual *value* of the data transferred is meaningless. The bits may be used to represent individual two-state conditions that are unrelated to the positional values of the bits. For example, a number of sensors could be connected to the Apple indicating conditions such as tank empty-or-full, heater on-or-off, value open-or-closed, and so on. A PEEK command could be used to input the status of these indicator bits, through an 8-bit input port. Thus, the value read from this input port might be 100, but the port is *sensing* eight individual on or off (logic one or logic zero) states, so the value of $100_{10}$ is meaningless. The individual binary bits each represent the state of an individual sensor. In this case:

$$100_{10} = 01100100_2$$

This indicates that three of the sensors are in the logic one state and five are in the logic zero state.

The POKE and PEEK commands can also be used in a similar manner to turn a device on or to turn a device off, based upon the state of the individual bits that have been sensed elsewhere in a control program. In fact, many of the I/O addresses used by the Apple are assigned to simple on/off devices such as the speaker. Thus, a simple command:

```
A = PEEK(49200)
```

will generate a "blip" on the speaker in the Apple. You should understand that the variable, A, is a "dummy," and its final value is not important, since the net effect of the simple BASIC statement is to pulse the speaker once. The speaker control command may be used in a loop to generate a low buzz from the speaker. This is shown in Example 1-4.

**Example 1-4. A Simple Speaker Control Program**

```
10  A = PEEK(49200)
20  GOTO 10
```

The important point to remember here is that the PEEK and POKE instructions are not limited simply to controlling the transfer of information on the data bus. They may also be used for specific control functions, such as pulsing a counter, turning on a pump, or tilting a solar collector.

## Assembly Language and BASIC

The BASIC-language programs that you write on your Apple computer bear very little relationship to the actual instructions that the 6502 microprocessor chip can actually execute. Each of your BASIC statements and commands is *interpreted* by the BASIC *interpreter* resident within the Apple computer. A programming manual for the 6502 chip, itself, would bear little relationship to the Apple software manual. The commands are very different.

The 6502 does not have a PRINT command, so it would not perform the following operation:

PRINT "THIS LOOKS LIKE FUN"

The BASIC interpreter determines that a PRINT operation is to take place and it then executes a series of assembly language program instructions that actually place the codes for the alphabetical characters in the display memory to spell out, "THIS LOOKS LIKE FUN." The assembly language steps consist of logic ones and zeros that cause the necessary internal and external 6502 operations to take place to transfer the message portion of the PRINT command to the display memory.

While we will not use assembly language programming to any extent in this book, you should be aware that it is the "base" computer language that causes the Apple to operate the way that it does.

The PEEK and POKE commands each cause many, many assembly language commands to be executed to produce the overall effect of data transfer. Since these BASIC language instructions must be interpreted, even when used one right after another, or in a loop, the *interpretation* software process can be slow. Two programs are shown in Example 1-5, both of which control the speaker in the Apple. Each series of program steps does the same thing; generating a tone on the speaker. Simply by listening to the differences in the two tones produced, you will be able to appreciate the difference in the speeds of execution of these programs.

Example 1-5. Comparison of Assembly Language and BASIC Programs for Speaker Control

| Basic Program | Assembly Language | |
|---|---|---|
| 10  A = PEEK(49200) | GO | LDY #$C0 |
| 20  GOTO 10 | LOOP | LDA #$0C |
| | | JSR WAIT |
| | | LDA SPKR |
| | | DEY |
| | | BNE LOOP |
| | | JMP GO |

The assembly language program generates a pleasing, even tone, while the BASIC program generates a low rumble. The assembly language program is similar to the one used by the Apple Monitor program where the internal WAIT subroutine has been used to generate a delay.

In some cases, assembly language programs have a *five-hundred to one* advantage over BASIC programs, although the BASIC programs are probably easier to write and debug. Assembly language programming is generally not recommended for the novice.

We will be mentioning assembly language programming very little, concentrating on the use of BASIC language programming instead. For further information on 6502 assembly language programming, we recommend *6502 Software Design* and *Programming and Interfacing the 6502, With Experiments* (Howard W. Sams & Co., Inc., Indianapolis, IN 46268).

## Binary and Decimal Numbering

The Apple computer system acquires, processes, and prints decimal (base-10) numbers. This makes it compatible with the numbering used by most people today. It would be difficult for us to readily understand and convert data values that were printed in a nondecimal format. The data and address lines are directly connected to the 6502 microprocessor chip, so they are binary, having only two states— a logic one or a logic zero. Thus, when we specify an I/O port address in a PEEK or POKE command, we must realize that the address (0-65535) will appear in its binary form on the address bus (0000000000000000-1111111111111111). You should be able to make the conversion between decimal and binary, in either direction.

Likewise, the data values transferred to and from the computer by the PEEK and POKE commands are also specified or acquired as 8-bit binary values, since the data bus is only eight bits "wide." The 8-bit data bus is a function of the data processing capability within the 6502 chip. It is *not* a function of the Apple. Thus, we are limited to 8-bit data transfers. Is this a great limitation? Generally not. In spite of it, the Apple can process a great deal of information, and, as you will see later, it is easy to interface to I/O devices.

One final note on addresses is necessary before leaving this chapter. The BASIC interpreter in the Apple computer has been set up to handle both *negative and positive* addresses. This does not mean that there are actually negative addresses in the computer. Can you imagine negative street numbers? The negative numbers are simple due to the way in which the *binary* equivalents of the addresses are stored in the Apple. Thus, the address for the speaker, 49200, is equivalent to −16336. To avoid confusion, we strongly recommend the use of the positive addresses. You can easily convert between negative and positive addresses simply by (a) adding 65536 to a negative address to yield the positive equivalent, or (b) by subtracting 65536 from the positive address to yield the negative equivalent. Both addresses, 49200 and −16336, generate the same 16-bit address, but we think that you will agree that negative addresses can seem a bit abstract and confusing.

# CHAPTER 2

# Apple Interfacing

At this point, you are probably wondering:

- How does the Apple actually transfer information to I/O devices?
- How are the I/O devices actually synchronized to the operation of the computer?
- How are individual I/O devices selected or identified?
- How do I/O devices place their data on the data bus and how do they actually receive it from the data bus?

These are important questions, since the answers to them will provide the basis for your understanding of microcomputer interfacing. We will be answering these questions in this and other chapters. We will also provide some experiments that will reinforce the concepts through hands-on experience.

A few examples of digital circuits will be provided in this chapter. We have assumed that you can "read" and interpret a logic circuit diagram, and that you are familiar with the more common SN7400-series transistor-transistor logic (TTL) circuits

## I/O DEVICE ADDRESS DECODING

Before we can discuss the actual transfer of information between I/O devices and the computer, we must first understand the circuitry and the signals that are used to identify or address the individual I/O devices. There are many schemes that may be used and we will examine several of them. It is impossible to show every possible scheme for addressing I/O devices, since modifications will be made to suit special needs.

When the Apple computer is programmed to perform a data transfer using either of the general-purpose I/O commands, PEEK or POKE, certain signals are generated by the 6502 processor to synchronize the flow of data. At this point, our main concern is the use of the address bus lines. These are the 16 lines that address individual memory locations and I/O devices. You should recall that the PEEK and POKE instructions each contain decimal address information that is used to identify the addressed memory location or I/O device. Of course, the Apple computer has no way of distinguishing between a memory location and an I/O port.

## DEVICE ADDRESSING

Each I/O device that is to be used with the computer must be able to recognize its own device address. Since the PEEK and POKE commands use 16-bit addresses, each I/O device must monitor these 16 address lines, A15-A0, for the occurrence of its address. There are three basic schemes that may be used by I/O device circuits to accomplish the monitoring for a specific address. These are:

- *Gating*–detecting a specific combination of logic signals.
- *Decoding*–a more flexible gating scheme in which many addresses may be detected.
- *Comparing*–comparing a preset or known address with the address-bus signals until a match occurs.

Combinations of these three techniques are possible and there are probably many variations that are possible. We will describe examples of each of the three basic address decoding schemes.

### Using Gates for Address Decoding

In the scheme for decoding device addresses in which individual gates are used, the address must be known so that the gates can be properly configured. In this example, we will use the device address $1010100011110111_2$ or $43255_{10}$. Since the binary notation is long, and somewhat cumbersome, you might feel more comfortable with the hexadecimal equivalent, A8F7H. Since NAND/AND gates are the predominant type of gating logic available, we will use these types of circuits in our logic.

To refresh your memory, the pin configurations for several types of AND/NAND gates are shown in Fig. 2-1, with the generalized truth table for a two-input AND gate and an equivalent NAND gate shown in Table 2-1. Since inverters such as the SN7404 are often found in device addressing circuits, a pin configuration for this chip has been included in Fig. 2-1. The truth tables in Table 2-1 also show the function of an inverter. *In all cases, the logic one state is the higher volt-*

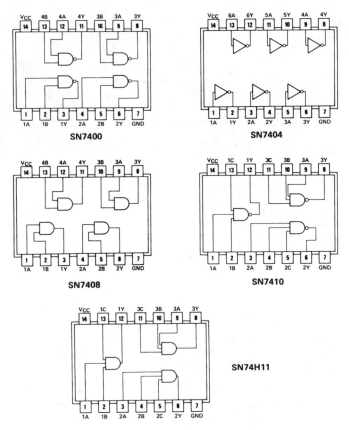

Fig. 2-1. Inverter and various AND/NAND gate pin configurations.

age (+2.8 to +5 volts) and the logic zero state is the lower voltage (0.0 to 0.8 volt). The NAND gate functions are available with 2, 3, 4, 8, and 13 inputs, while the AND gates are available with 2, 3, or 4 inputs.

Since the unique output state, logic one for an AND gate and logic zero for a NAND gate, occurs only when *all* of the inputs to an AND or a NAND gate are all logic ones, we will have to configure the binary address $1010100011110111_2$ so that it generated 16 logic ones at the input to the AND or NAND gate, when it is present on the 16-bit address bus. You have probably realized that there are no 16-input AND or NAND gates available commercially, so some other configuration must be used instead. It is very easy to use a separate 8-input NAND gate to detect a pattern of binary address bits on the high-address bus (A15-A8), and another 8-input NAND gate to detect a pattern of binary bits on the low-address bus (A7-A0). Simple inverter func-

| AND Gate | | NAND Gate | | Inverter | |
|---|---|---|---|---|---|
| Inputs | Output | Inputs | Output | Input | Output |
| A  B | Q | A  B | Q | A | Q |
| 0  0 | 0 | 0  0 | 1 | 0 | 1 |
| 0  1 | 0 | 0  1 | 1 | 1 | 0 |
| 1  0 | 0 | 1  0 | 1 | | |
| 1  1 | 1 | 1  1 | 0 | | |

tions are used to invert the logic zero address bits so that they apply
logic ones to their corresponding gate inputs, as shown in Fig. 2-2.
In this circuit, two inverters and a NAND gate have been used to combine the output from each of the 8-input NAND gates, so that the output of the circuit will be a logic zero only when the *complete* pattern
of 16 bits, $1010100011110111_2$, is detected on the 16-bit address bus.

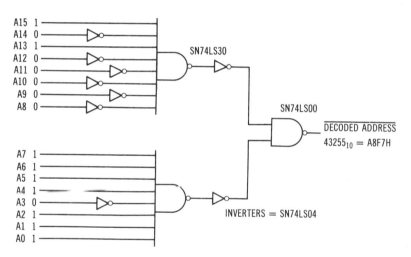

Fig. 2-2. Gating circuit used to decode address 43255 or A8F7H.

One of the disadvantages of this circuit is that some of the address
signals must go through four gates before reaching the decoded address output from the 2-input NAND gate. Since each gate delays the
signal slightly, this might cause some timing problems in the circuit.
Actually, the time delays are fairly minor, and we will ignore them
for now. The delay can be reduced somewhat by using a NOR or OR
gate in the circuit to combine the outputs from the two 8-input NAND
gates. This is good design practice. NOR and OR gates are readily
available and are used quite extensively in computer interfacing. A

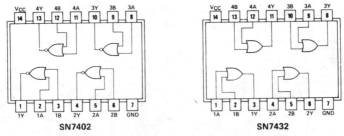

Fig. 2-3. Typical NOR and OR gate IC pin configurations.

typical NOR and OR gate are shown in Fig. 2-3, with the corresponding truth tables provided in Table 2-2.

While the gating scheme shown in Fig. 2-2 is effective in decoding a single address, and relatively inexpensive, it is inflexible. A more flexible approach is shown in Fig. 2-4. This circuit illustrates the use of a gating scheme in which inverters may be used to invert individual address bits, as required. The bits may also be used without inversion. The jumpers allow the device address to be preset, as illustrated in Fig. 2-5. In this circuit, only the low-address bus gating has been shown, for clarity. A duplicate gating circuit is required for the high-address bus lines. In this type of a gating circuit, any one of the 65536 possible addresses may be selected, but only one at a time.

The programmable gating circuit provides broad flexibility, in that addresses are easily changed to meet specific requirements for an interface, but such a circuit can select only a single address, and this is a severe limitation. When several I/O devices are located on the same circuit board, each will require its own address gating circuit. This limitation can be overcome with other addressing schemes.

Unfortunately, the gating schemes that we have shown are not all that is required to uniquely address and control an I/O device. You should recall from the discussion of the READ/$\overline{\text{WRITE}}$ (R/$\overline{\text{W}}$) signal in the previous chapter, that the R/$\overline{\text{W}}$ signal is used to synchronize the flow of information to and from the computer. The I/O devices must also use this control signal, if they are to use the data bus properly. In many interfaces that are designed for 6502-based com-

Table 2-2. Truth Tables for a Two-Input NOR Gate and OR Gate

| NOR Gate | | | OR Gate | | |
|---|---|---|---|---|---|
| Inputs | | Output | Inputs | | Output |
| A | B | Q | A | B | Q |
| 0 | 0 | 1 | 0 | 0 | 0 |
| 0 | 1 | 0 | 0 | 1 | 1 |
| 1 | 0 | 0 | 1 | 0 | 1 |
| 1 | 1 | 0 | 1 | 1 | 1 |

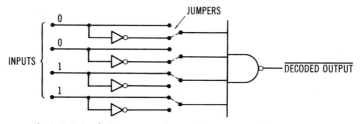

Fig. 2-4. A simple 4-input gate that can be programmed for 1's and 0's.

puter systems, the R/$\overline{W}$ line is used to provide the logic-zero write pulse, with the R/$\overline{W}$ signal being *inverted* to generate a separate read pulse. The two resulting control signals, $\overline{\text{WRITE}}$ ($\overline{\text{WR}}$) and $\overline{\text{READ}}$ ($\overline{\text{RD}}$), are easy to use in interface circuits, since they are active in the logic zero state. The use of these signals is shown in Fig. 2-6. In this circuit, the output from the 16-bit gating circuit is combined with $\overline{\text{RD}}$ and $\overline{\text{WR}}$ to provide two signals for I/O port control. These two control signals are a combination of the decoded address and the $\overline{\text{WRITE}}$ pulse, and a combination of the decoded address and the $\overline{\text{READ}}$ pulse. The resulting pulse from each gate is called an *address select pulse,* or a *device select pulse.* More generally, a *decoded address* is gated with a *function pulse* ($\overline{\text{RD}}$ or $\overline{\text{WR}}$) to generate a *device select pulse.* In the circuit diagram shown in Fig. 2-6, the $\overline{\text{RD}}$ 49280 pulse could be used to control an input port, while the WR 49280 pulse could be used to control an output port. Note that the notation for the WR 49280 pulse does not have a "bar" over it.

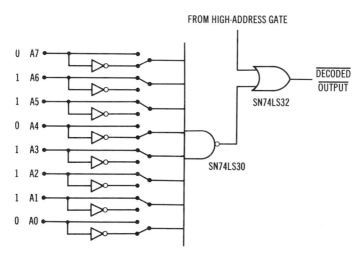

Fig. 2-5. Programmable gate used for device address decoding. (High address section is equivalent.)

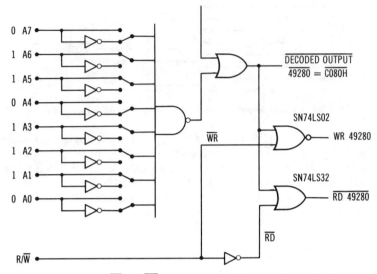

Fig. 2-6. Using $\overline{RD}$ and $\overline{WR}$ signals to generate device select pulses for device synchronization.

This means that the pulse is active in the logic one state, while the $\overline{RD}$ 49280 pulse is active in the logic zero state. In this example, it is quite proper to note the address on the I/O ports by using a hexadecimal value, for example, $\overline{RD}$ C080H.

Before going further, you should be sure that you understand that a *reading operation* involves *reading information into the computer* from an input port, while a *writing operation* involves the *transfer of information from the computer* to an external device. It is also quite proper and useful to use one address to control an input port and an output port. Since the $\overline{RD}$ and $\overline{WR}$ pulses cannot be coincident, there is no conflict between an input port and an output port that have been assigned the same address. You *cannot* assign two input ports the same address, and you *should not* assign two output ports the same address. In fact, you may find that even though an input port and an output port have been assigned the same address, they may be unrelated as to their function, and may be used on separate interface circuits.

The concepts and the basic circuits that have been developed in this section are very important and they will be carried forward to other sections and chapters. It is important that you understand the use of the signals that have been discussed to select devices. We have not yet discussed what these input and output devices are, or how they work, but we shall discuss this in the next chapter.

## Using Decoders

In many cases, it is easier to use *decoder* circuits in place of the gate address detecting circuits, and, in some cases, in place of the NOR-gate device select circuits, too. Why are decoders so useful? Perhaps it is best to take a look at several types of decoders to see what they look like and how they operate. As you examine the decoder circuits, keep in mind that they are simply collections of gates that have been "integrated" into an easy-to-use decoder circuit.

Decoder circuits are generally specified as *x-line to y-line* decoders, where *x* represents the number of binary inputs, say four inputs, and where *y* represents the number of possible outputs, or the number of different binary states present on the *x* inputs. Thus, for the four inputs, there would be 16 possible outputs, creating a 4-line to 16-line decoder or a 4- to 16-line decoder. This is, in fact, a real decoder circuit, as you will see.

Each of the binary inputs has two states, a logic one and a logic zero. These inputs are independent of one another. The outputs are also binary, in the sense that they have two possible values, but they are *not independent*. There will only be *one* unique output from the decoder, representing the value or "weight" present at the binary inputs. In most cases, the unique output state is a logic zero, with the other outputs in their logic one state.

A typical decoder integrated circuit is the SN74LS139. This integrated circuit actually contains two independent two-line to four-line decoders, as shown in Fig. 2-7.

The truth table for the SN74LS139 is shown in Table 2-3.

Of course, the truth table applies to both of the decoders within the SN74LS139 integrated-circuit package, or "chip." Most decoder circuits incorporate an enabling input, so that the decoder may be

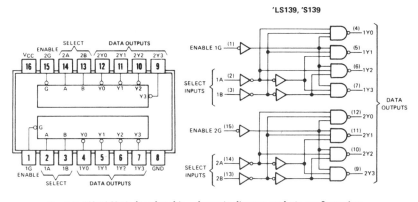

Fig. 2-7. SN74LS139 decoder chip schematic diagram and pin configuration.

## Table 2-3. Truth Table for an SN74LS139 Decoder

| Inputs | | | Outputs | | | |
|:---:|:---:|:---:|:---:|:---:|:---:|:---:|
| Enable | Select | | | | | |
| G | B | A | Y0 | Y1 | Y2 | Y3 |
| H | X | X | H | H | H | H |
| L | L | L | L | H | H | H |
| L | L | H | H | L | H | H |
| L | H | L | H | H | L | H |
| L | H | H | H | H | H | L |

H = high level      L = low level      X = irrelevant (don't care)

turned on or turned off by one logic input. This is the function of the ENABLE or "G" input on each of the decoders in the SN74LS139. Note that when the "G" input is a logic one, all of the outputs are forced into the logic one state, regardless of the states of the A and B inputs. This allows the decoder to be gated on or off. In the off state, the power is not removed, but the outputs are all forced into the logic one state.

Let us now examine a simple, rather trivial, example of the use of a two-line to four-line decoder for device address decoding. We will assume that we only have a few I/O devices, so that the decoders in the SN74LS139 decoder package can handle our needs. A typical decoder circuit is shown in Fig. 2-8. In this circuit, only two address bits have been decoded, the rest have been ignored. Note that the enable input has been grounded so that the outputs of the decoder will operate properly. The added NOR and OR gates generate the actual device select pulses.

The device select signals have been noted as RD X, RD Y, and WR Y, since there is no *specific* address that will actuate each. Addresses 01010101 00000010, 00011101 11110110 and 00000000 11111110 will all cause the RD X device select pulse to be generated, if they are

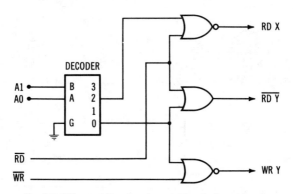

Fig. 2-8. 2-Line-to-4-line decoder used for device addressing.

used in PEEK commands, for example A=PEEK(21762). This *non-absolute* device addressing results because address bits A15-A2 have not been used in the decoding scheme. Nonabsolute addressing means that there are several addresses that will actuate the selected device. The circuit shown in Fig. 2-8 will decode four addresses and thus eight individual devices may be selected, four input devices and four output devices; additional NOR gates or OR gates are required, though. In a small system, this may be adequate, although the decoding scheme does not provide a great deal of flexibility in allowing the addition of new I/O devices beyond the original eight. Although this scheme is not very flexible, let's take a closer look at it, since it allows us to develop two other concepts that can be applied to other decoder schemes.

In Fig. 2-8, the enable input, "G," of the decoder is simply grounded, to always enable the decoding action. This input can allow the decoder to be used for absolute decoding. A gating circuit can be used to supply an enabling signal to the decoder only when a preset pattern of address bits, on address lines A15-A2, is present. You have already seen the use of multiple-input gating circuits; the circuit in Fig. 2-5 is a good example. This circuit can be readily adapted to provide the enable input for a simple decoder. Since the A1 and A0 inputs are being used as inputs to the decoder, they are not used as inputs to the gating circuit that provides the decoder-enabling signal. A simple example of this is shown in Fig. 2-9. In this circuit, the ADDRESS ENABLE signal is generated by a gating circuit (Fig. 2-5). In this case, the jumpers associated with the A1 and A0 address inputs are simply disconnected.

If we assume that the high-address gating circuit has been preset for an address bit pattern of 11110000, and that the A1 and A0 inputs to the circuit have been disconnected (see Fig. 2-5), then the decoder shown in Fig. 2-9 will only be enabled for addresses 11110000 01101100 through 11110000 01101111. Thus, in this circuit, the de-

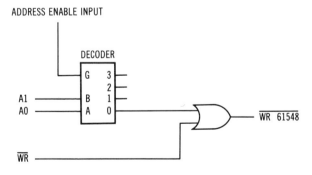

**Fig. 2-9. Decoder used for absolute address selection.**

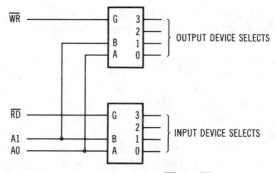

Fig. 2-10. Decoder enable inputs used with $\overline{\text{WR}}$ and $\overline{\text{RD}}$ to generate device select signals.

coder outputs of 0, 1, 2, and 3 correspond to device addresses 61,548 through 61,551, or F06CH through F06FH. Only the $\overline{\text{WR}}$ 61548 device select pulse has been generated in this example. Again, an OR gate or a NOR gate is required for each device select pulse that is to be generated.

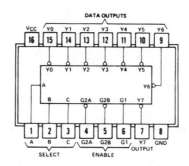

'LS138, 'S138

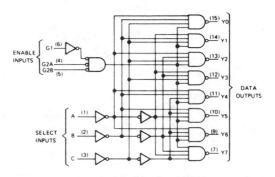

Fig. 2-11. SN74LS138 decoder.

An alternate approach is to use both of the decoder circuits in the SN74LS139 chip, using the $\overline{RD}$ and $\overline{WR}$ function pulses to enable the decoders. In this way, the address selection is again nonabsolute, but the device select gating is performed within the chip. This is shown in Fig. 2-10. The NOR and OR gates are no longer required for each device select pulse to be generated. While this circuit may not be immediately useful, it does illustrate the use of the enable input of the decoder to generate the device select pulse. The decoder gating or enabling input may be used for device select pulse generation, or for absolute decoding. In some cases, it may be used for both.

### Large Decoders

There are additional decoder circuits that will be useful to you in interfacing your Apple computer to external devices. These decod-

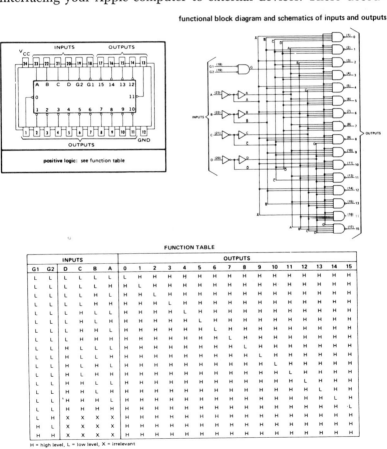

functional block diagram and schematics of inputs and outputs

positive logic: see function table

**FUNCTION TABLE**

| INPUTS | | | | | | OUTPUTS | | | | | | | | | | | | | | | |
|---|---|---|---|---|---|---|---|---|---|---|---|---|---|---|---|---|---|---|---|---|---|
| G1 | G2 | D | C | B | A | 0 | 1 | 2 | 3 | 4 | 5 | 6 | 7 | 8 | 9 | 10 | 11 | 12 | 13 | 14 | 15 |
| L | L | L | L | L | L | L | H | H | H | H | H | H | H | H | H | H | H | H | H | H | H |
| L | L | L | L | L | H | H | L | H | H | H | H | H | H | H | H | H | H | H | H | H | H |
| L | L | L | L | H | L | H | H | L | H | H | H | H | H | H | H | H | H | H | H | H | H |
| L | L | L | L | H | H | H | H | H | L | H | H | H | H | H | H | H | H | H | H | H | H |
| L | L | L | H | L | L | H | H | H | H | L | H | H | H | H | H | H | H | H | H | H | H |
| L | L | L | H | L | H | H | H | H | H | H | L | H | H | H | H | H | H | H | H | H | H |
| L | L | L | H | H | L | H | H | H | H | H | H | L | H | H | H | H | H | H | H | H | H |
| L | L | L | H | H | H | H | H | H | H | H | H | H | L | H | H | H | H | H | H | H | H |
| L | L | H | L | L | L | H | H | H | H | H | H | H | H | L | H | H | H | H | H | H | H |
| L | L | H | L | L | H | H | H | H | H | H | H | H | H | H | L | H | H | H | H | H | H |
| L | L | H | L | H | L | H | H | H | H | H | H | H | H | H | H | L | H | H | H | H | H |
| L | L | H | L | H | H | H | H | H | H | H | H | H | H | H | H | H | L | H | H | H | H |
| L | L | H | H | L | L | H | H | H | H | H | H | H | H | H | H | H | H | L | H | H | H |
| L | L | H | H | L | H | H | H | H | H | H | H | H | H | H | H | H | H | H | L | H | H |
| L | L | H | H | H | L | H | H | H | H | H | H | H | H | H | H | H | H | H | H | L | H |
| L | L | H | H | H | H | H | H | H | H | H | H | H | H | H | H | H | H | H | H | H | L |
| L | H | X | X | X | X | H | H | H | H | H | H | H | H | H | H | H | H | H | H | H | H |
| H | L | X | X | X | X | H | H | H | H | H | H | H | H | H | H | H | H | H | H | H | H |
| H | H | X | X | X | X | H | H | H | H | H | H | H | H | H | H | H | H | H | H | H | H |

H = high level, L = low level, X = irrelevant

**Fig. 2-12. SN74154 decoder.**

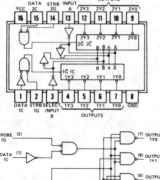

Fig. 2-13. SN74155 decoder.

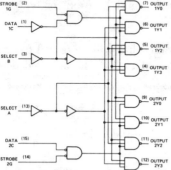

**FUNCTION TABLES**
**2-LINE-TO-4-LINE DECODER**
**OR 1-LINE-TO-4-LINE DEMULTIPLEXER**

| SELECT | | STROBE | DATA | OUTPUTS | | | |
|---|---|---|---|---|---|---|---|
| B | A | 1G | 1C | 1Y0 | 1Y1 | 1Y2 | 1Y3 |
| X | X | H | X | H | H | H | H |
| L | L | L | H | L | H | H | H |
| L | H | L | H | H | L | H | H |
| H | L | L | H | H | H | L | H |
| H | H | L | H | H | H | H | L |
| X | X | X | L | H | H | H | H |

| SELECT | | STROBE | DATA | OUTPUTS | | | |
|---|---|---|---|---|---|---|---|
| B | A | 2G | 2C | 2Y0 | 2Y1 | 2Y2 | 2Y3 |
| X | X | H | X | H | H | H | H |
| L | L | L | L | L | H | H | H |
| L | H | L | L | H | L | H | H |
| H | L | L | L | H | H | L | H |
| H | H | L | L | H | H | H | L |
| X | X | X | H | H | H | H | H |

ers, depending on the type you choose, may have additional inputs, enable lines, and outputs. Examples are shown in Fig. 2-11 for the SN74LS138 decoder and in Fig. 2-12 for the SN74154 decoder. The SN75155 decoder has also been included ( Fig. 2-13) since it has two

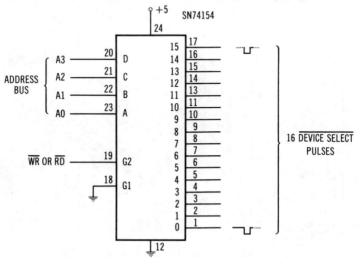

Fig. 2-14. SN74154 decoder used to produce 16 nonabsolute decoded device select pulses.

sections, but the address inputs, A and B, are common to both of the decoder sections. Each section of the SN74155 has separate control or enabling inputs.

A large decoder such as the SN74154 4-line to 16-line decoder provides broad address decoding flexibility. A single SN74154 decoder may be used to nonabsolutely decode 16 addresses, and when either WR or RD is used as one of the enable inputs, the SN75154 may be used to directly generate 16 device select pulses, without the need for additional gating. This is shown in Fig. 2-14.

Additional decoders or gates may be added to the basic circuit so that absolutely decoded device select pulses are generated. A typical example of this is shown in Fig. 2-15. Either the $\overline{RD}$ or $\overline{WR}$ signal may be used to gate or enable the lower decoder. The NOR gates have been used to gate together the *address selection signal* from the upper portion of the circuit and the *address selection plus the function pulse* from the lower decoder. Thus, the upper portion of the circuit is used to "qualify" the outputs from the lower decoder to make the address selection absolute. In this example, two device select pulses have been shown. Although this circuit will work, it is not particularly useful, since it can be simplified.

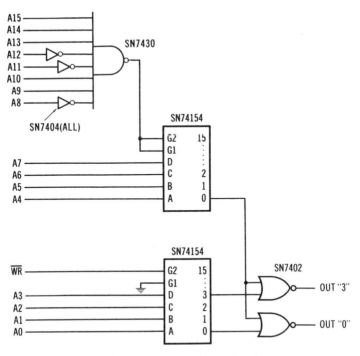

Fig. 2-15. Using SN74154 decoders and gating for absolute device address selection.

Since the SN74154 decoders have two enabling inputs, G1 and G2, the NOR gates shown in Fig. 2-15 may be eliminated by using the second enabling input as the "qualifier" that will enable the decoder. The use of this type of circuit is shown in Fig. 2-16. In this example, the lower decoder now has two enabling input signals, the $\overline{\text{RD}}$ control signal from the computer, and the enabling signal from the upper portion of the circuit. You should note that the upper decoder has both of its enabling inputs used, so that it is enabled only for a specific pattern of bits on the HI address bus. In this case, gating has been used to generate the enabling signal for the upper decoder.

A third decoder could be added to this circuit to generate device select pulses for output devices. The inputs to this additional decoder would be the same as those to the lower decoder, except that the $\overline{\text{WR}}$ signal would be used instead of the $\overline{\text{RD}}$ signal.

Many decoder schemes are possible, and you will have an opportunity to explore the use of decoders in the experiments. The main point is that the use of decoders simplifies the process of device selection and gating. Decoders are generally used in situations that require flexibility and the generation of several device select or device address signals in proximity to one another.

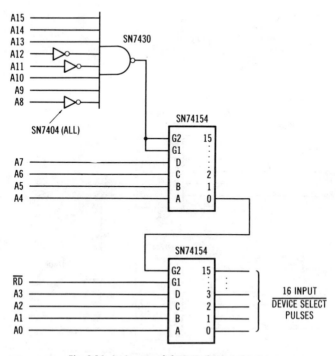

Fig. 2-16. An improved device selection circuit.

FUNCTION TABLES

| COMPARING INPUTS | | | | CASCADING INPUTS | | | OUTPUTS | | |
|---|---|---|---|---|---|---|---|---|---|
| A3, B3 | A2, B2 | A1, B1 | A0, B0 | A > B | A < B | A = B | A > B | A < B | A = B |
| A3 > B3 | X | X | X | X | X | X | H | L | L |
| A3 < B3 | X | X | X | X | X | X | L | H | L |
| A3 = B3 | A2 > B2 | X | X | X | X | X | H | L | L |
| A3 = B3 | A2 < B2 | X | X | X | X | X | L | H | L |
| A3 = B3 | A2 = B2 | A1 > B1 | X | X | X | X | H | L | L |
| A3 = B3 | A2 = B2 | A1 < B1 | X | X | X | X | L | H | L |
| A3 = B3 | A2 = B2 | A1 = B1 | A0 > B0 | X | X | X | H | L | L |
| A3 = B3 | A2 = B2 | A1 = B1 | A0 < B0 | X | X | X | L | H | L |
| A3 = B3 | A2 = B2 | A1 = B1 | A0 = B0 | H | L | L | H | L | L |
| A3 = B3 | A2 = B2 | A1 = B1 | A0 = B0 | L | H | L | L | H | L |
| A3 = B3 | A2 = B2 | A1 = B1 | A0 = B0 | L | L | H | L | L | H |

'85, 'LS85, 'S85

| | | | | | | | | | |
|---|---|---|---|---|---|---|---|---|---|
| A3 = B3 | A2 = B2 | A1 = B1 | A0 = B0 | X | X | H | L | L | H |
| A3 = B3 | A2 = B2 | A1 = B1 | A0 = B0 | H | H | L | L | L | L |
| A3 = B3 | A2 = B2 | A1 = B1 | A0 = B0 | L | L | L | H | H | L |

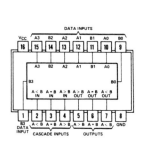

Fig. 2-17. SN7485 four-bit magnitude comparator chip.

## Using Comparators

The use of digital comparators for device address detection will be the last technique discussed. The comparator-based schemes are relatively straightforward and they are very similar to the "programmable-gate" schemes shown in Figs. 2-4 and 2-5. Remember that comparators, too, are simply collections of gates, connected or integrated, to perform a comparing function. The comparator circuits allow us to present an address that is constantly compared to the 16-

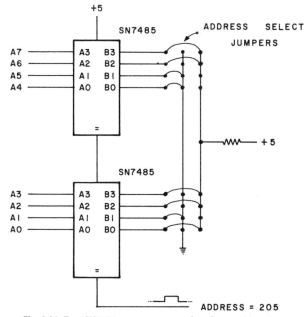

Fig. 2-18. Two SN7485 comparators used to detect address 205.

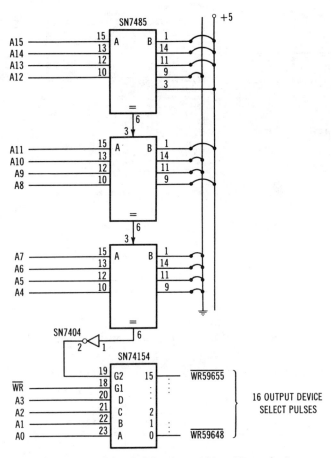

Fig. 2-19. Comparators and decoders used for address selection.

bit values on the address bus. This comparing is done by gating circuits within the comparator chips. A typical comparator is the SN7485 4-bit magnitude comparator, shown in Fig. 2-17. Besides the equal condition, the SN7485 can also detect the greater-than and less-than conditions, but these are not used in address comparison. Caution: *The SN74L85 version of the SN7485 chip is not a pin-for-pin equivalent.* Consult a manufacturer's data sheet for additional information.

A typical address-comparison scheme is shown in Fig. 2-18 in which only 8 of the 16 address bits have been shown for clarity. The comparators have been preset to detect the address 205 or $11001101_2$. Like an 8-input gate circuit, this scheme can only detect a single address, so most comparators are used with decoders for a flexible decoding scheme, as shown in Fig. 2-19. The unique "equal condition" output of the SN7485 comparators is a logic one, so where necessary, it has been inverted to provide the enabling signal to a decoder chip. In this circuit, two additional comparators have been used so that the device addresses are absolutely decoded. Now, the outputs of the SN74154 decoder are only active when address bits A15-A4 match the corresponding logic states that have been preset at the inputs to the three comparator circuits. In this case, the address bits must be 11101001 for A15-A8 and 0000 for A7-A4. Since the $\overline{WR}$ function pulse must also be present to enable the decoder, you should realize that output device address selection signals are being generated by this circuit, for addresses 59648 through 59655, or E900H through E907H. Another SN74154 decoder could be added to this circuit to generate 16 device address selection signals for input devices. You would need parallel connections between the inputs of both decoders except that the $\overline{RD}$ signal would be used in place of the $\overline{WR}$ signal.

This completes our discussion of device addressing circuits and the combinations of device addresses and function pulses to obtain device select pulses. In future examples, we will expect that you will recognize the notation $\overline{WR}$ 54390 as a logic-zero device select pulse, generated by the proper gating of the $\overline{WR}$ function pulse and address 54390. In some cases, the actual gating will be shown, but in most cases, we will assume that you understand the origin of the signal. While you will probably see many different device addressing and selecting circuits in other books, magazine articles, etc., you will quickly find that they all function in pretty much the same way— gating an address signal with a function pulse to select a particular device.

In some of the experiments, you will explore the use of device select pulses to control devices. In the next chapter, you will learn how these pulses are used to control the flow of 8-bit data bytes on the data bus of the 6502.

# CHAPTER 3

# I/O Interfacing

Now that we have developed a number of ways of selecting and identifying I/O devices, the actual construction and configuration of the I/O ports become very important. In this section, we will develop some of the actual bus interfacing schemes that will allow I/O devices to transfer 8-bit bytes to the computer and to receive bytes transferred to them by the computer. As we found with the device selecting circuits, there are many circuits for input ports and output ports. Only a few sample circuits will be provided to illustrate the basic principles of interfacing.

## OUTPUT PORTS

Output ports are devices that receive data bytes from the computer, controlled by POKE commands in the BASIC-language programs. You have already seen that there is a definite timing relationship between data on the bus, the $\overline{\text{WR}}$ pulse and the device address, when a POKE command is executed. This has been shown in Fig. 1-4. In the Apple computer, the duration of the $\overline{\text{WR}}$ pulse is about 500 nanoseconds. If we use the $\overline{\text{WR}}$ pulse to gate the data from the data bus to an output device, through the use of the device select pulse, the data is only presented to the output device for about 500 nanoseconds. This period is hardly long enough to allow the receiving device to perform a meaningful function. To eliminate this problem, each output port must be equipped with some sort of circuit that can acquire data from the bus and "hold" it for as long as needed, or until it is "updated" by another data transfer.

The type of circuit that can perform this function is called a *latch*, since it can latch the information and hold it until it is updated or until the power is turned off. There are many different types of latch integrated circuits that offer different configurations of control and data inputs and outputs. Rather than describe all of the various types of latches, we have chosen to describe three general-purpose devices, the SN7475, the SN74175, and the SN74LS373. The pin configurations and function tables are shown in Fig. 3-1. While the SN7475 and SN74LS373 are true latch devices, the SN74175 really contains flip-flops. The SN7475 latch chip contains four latch circuits and the SN74175 contains four flip-flop circuits, so two SN7475 or two SN74175 chips are required for each 8-bit output port. The SN74LS373 contains eight latch circuits, so only one of these is required to construct an 8-bit output port.

Let us briefly describe the operation of these latch circuits, so that their use becomes apparent. We will use the SN7475 latch chip as an example. The SN7475 latch circuits can be thought of as "gates that remember." This is shown in the function table for the SN7475 latch, shown in Fig. 3-1. In examining this function table, you will note that when the enable input (G) is a logic one, the data, or logic level present at the "D" input, is passed through the latch to the "Q" output. The $\overline{Q}$ output is the inversion of the Q output. When the enable input goes from a logic one to a logic zero, the level present at the D input at this time is latched or remembered by the Q and $\overline{Q}$ outputs. The timing relationship shown in Fig. 3-2 illustrates these operations.

As soon as the "G" input goes to the logic one level, the Q output assumes the state of the "D" input even if the levels at the "D" input are changing. The logic levels are passed from the "D" input to the "Q" output when the "G" input is a logic one; the "Q" output remains at the level of the "D" input when the "G" input goes to a logic zero. The SN7475 is divided into two sections, each of which can operate independently of the other. The two gate inputs may be connected to make the four latch circuits operate in tandem. Of course, the inputs and the outputs to the latches remain independent, so that four input signals may originate from different places in a circuit. However, all four inputs will be latched at the same time if the separate functions are operated in tandem.

The SN74LS373 operates in the same way as the SN7475, although only one gating or enabling signal is used. In this chip, only the Q outputs are provided. The $\overline{Q}$ outputs are not available. An additional output control has been provided, but when the SN74LS373 is used as an output port, this control signal, Output Control (pin 1), is usually grounded.

The SN74175 chip contains four flip-flops that acquire and hold information that is present on the *positive-going edge* of the clock pulse. The outputs are only updated at this time, and the inputs are

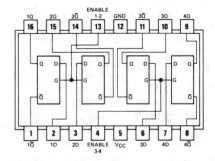

**FUNCTION TABLE**
(Each Latch)

| INPUTS | | OUTPUTS | |
|---|---|---|---|
| D | G | Q | $\bar{Q}$ |
| L | H | L | H |
| H | H | H | L |
| X | L | $Q_0$ | $\bar{Q}_0$ |

H = high level, L = low level, X = irrelevant
$Q_0$ = the level of Q before the high-to-low transition of G

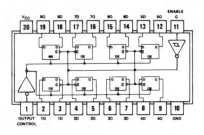

'LS373, 'S373
**FUNCTION TABLE**

| OUTPUT CONTROL | ENABLE G | D | OUTPUT |
|---|---|---|---|
| L | H | H | H |
| L | H | L | L |
| L | L | X | $Q_0$ |
| H | X | X | Z |

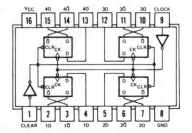

**FUNCTION TABLE**
(EACH FLIP-FLOP)

| INPUTS | | | OUTPUTS | |
|---|---|---|---|---|
| CLEAR | CLOCK | D | Q | $\bar{Q}$ t |
| L | X | X | L | H |
| H | ↑ | H | H | L |
| H | ↑ | L | L | H |
| H | L | X | $Q_0$ | $\bar{Q}_0$ |

Fig. 3-1. Pin configurations and function tables for SN7475 (top), SN74LS373 (middle), and SN74175 (bottom) latch chips.

not continuously gated through the SN74175 on either the logic zero or the logic one portion of the clock signal. This is what distinguishes this flip-flop device from the latch devices, although in computer interfacing, the net effect of both types of chips is the same.

A common clear input is also provided on the SN74175, so that the flip-flops may be "cleared" ($Q=0$, $\bar{Q}=1$), when this input is taken to

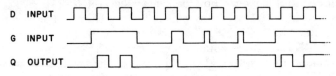

Fig. 3-2. SN7475 latch circuit timing relationships.

the logic zero state. In most cases, the clear input will be connected to +5 volts (logic one) and will not be used.

Each of the integrated circuits may be used to latch and maintain the data put out by the Apple computer during the execution of a POKE command. It is a simple matter of using an output device select pulse to activate the latch circuit once it has been properly connected to the bus. A typical 8-bit output port is shown in Fig. 3-3. In this circuit, a logic one output device select pulse is required to cause the latch circuits to acquire and hold the information output by the Apple.

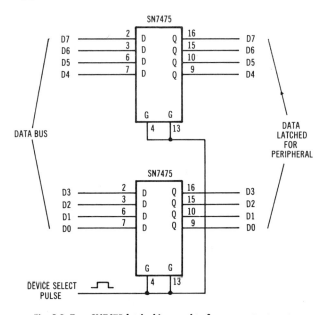

Fig. 3-3. Two SN7475 latch chips used to form an output port.

In Fig. 3-4, two SN74175 latch chips have been used as an output port, with some sort of logic monitors being used to provide a visual indication of the information that has been latched by the chips. The "1" indication at the connections to the CLEAR inputs at the output port means that these inputs are connected to +5 volts, or a logic one level. The "1" notation is used to distinguish a logic level connection from a power-supplying connection, which is noted as +5 volts, or +5 V.

An SN74LS373 8-bit or *octal* latch has been used as an output port as shown in Fig. 3-5. Only one integrated circuit is required for this output port. The Output Control line has been grounded so that the outputs are permanently enabled. Again, an output device select

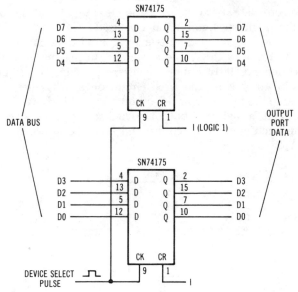

Fig. 3-4. Two SN74175 latch chips used to form an output port.

pulse must be supplied from the device selection logic. Once an output port has been properly connected to the data bus and a source for the device select pulse, it can be accessed under control of software commands. For example, the command, POKE 49312,0 would transfer the value zero to the output port with the address 49312. If there is actually an output port connected to the data bus, which corresponds to this address, then the value zero would be transferred to it.

The program shown in Example 3-1 may be used to generate an increasing binary count at output port 49320. The count will con-

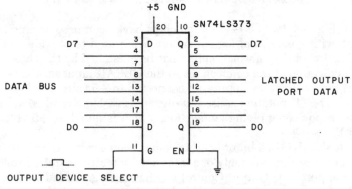

Fig. 3-5. SN74LS373 latch chip used to form an output port.

tinue in sequence (in binary), 255, 255, 0, 1, 2 . . . 254, 255, 0, 1, etc. This program will be seen again, in the experiments.

**Example 3-1. An 8-Bit Binary Counting Program for Port 49320**

```
10   FOR N = 0 TO 255
20   POKE 49320,N
30   NEXT N
40   GOTO 10
```

Output ports are rather easy to construct. Most parallel-in, parallel-out logic devices with internal latch capabilities can be used as latches. Examples of devices that can be used as latches are the SN74193 programmable binary counter, the SN74LS194A universal shift register, the SN74198 shift register, etc.

Most output ports are readily configured with standard integrated circuits, but some of the newer integrated-circuit devices that are meant specifically for use with microcomputers are becoming available with built-in latch functions. An example is the Signetics NE5018 8-bit digital-to-analog converter chip which contains a latch section.

Typical applications for output ports include the following:

Transfer data to a printer
Transfer data to a video display
Control a traffic light
Transfer data to a floppy disk
Actuate switches on a model railroad
Control valves and pumps in a chemical process
Control a plotter
Transfer data to a seven-segment display
Control another computer

In some applications, the value of the information is actually used, while in others, the on or off state of each bit is used. Some devices such as a printer may use a combination: ports for the transfer of the data to be printed and ports for the control of the printer functions. Displays made up of seven-segment LEDs frequently require the use of several output ports, even though the display is considered to be only one "device."

## INPUT PORTS

Input ports are used with I/O devices so that they may transfer information to the computer in 8-bit bytes. Unlike output ports that must be able to accept and hold information that is placed on the bus at a specific time, and may be continuously connected to the data bus, input ports must be able to "disconnect" themselves from the

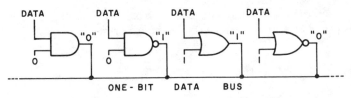

DATA      DATA      DATA      DATA

"0"      "1"      "1"      "0"

0      0      I      I

ONE - BIT    DATA    BUS

**Fig. 3-6. Attempted use of standard gates on a data bus.**

bus when they are not in use. The input ports must pass logic ones and zeros to the CPU, but they must be configured so that they do not interfere with the use of the bus when they are not selected.

Depending on the type of gate chosen, simple gates cannot be used to gate data onto the data bus lines since their "unselected" output state will be either a logic one or a logic zero, as shown in Fig. 3-6. Note that even when none of the gates is selected or enabled, the outputs of the gates are at different logic levels, as noted by the quoted logic levels. These levels "compete" for the use of the bus, probably leading to one or more burned out chips. This should clearly illustrate why gates alone are not used on data buses.

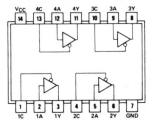

**Fig. 3-7. SN74125 bus buffer chip
pin configuration.**

Special integrated circuits with *three-state* outputs are available to simplify the design of input ports. A typical three-state device is the SN74125 bus buffer, shown in Fig. 3-7. The diagram of the four devices should look familiar. It is simply a buffer (logic one in, logic one out, etc.), but with an additional control line, shown connected to one of the angular sides of the buffer symbol. The buffer will pass logic ones and zeros from its input to its output when it is enabled, but unlike a simple gate, when it is disabled, the output appears to be electrically disconnected from the bus, or other logic device, to which it is connected. In three-state devices, this third state is often called the HI-Z or high-impedance state, to note its disconnected condition. The disconnecting and connecting is rapid, generally taking less than 20 nanoseconds.

In the SN74125 circuit, each three-state buffer has its own enable input, which must be a logic zero for the data to be passed from the input to the output. A logic one state on the enable input forces the output into the high-impedance state. A similar integrated circuit,

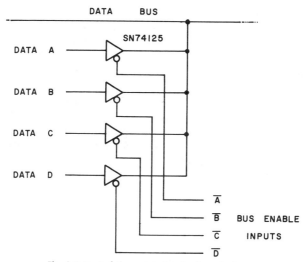

Fig. 3-8. Typical three-state bus for four devices.

the SN74126, is a pin-for-pin replacement for the SN74125, except that it is enabled with a logic one and disabled with a logic zero. These chips serve to illustrate the action of three-state devices, but they are not generally found in computer interface circuits, since more useful devices are available.

For purposes of illustration, a typical bus is shown in Fig. 3-8. In this circuit, four one-bit devices have been connected to the bus. Only a one-bit bus is shown for clarity, although in an 8-bit bus system, eight lines would be required. When one of the BUS ENABLE INPUTS is placed in the logic zero state, the corresponding data bit is passed through the buffer and onto the bus. We will assume that there are no other devices connected to the bus. Thus, the truth table shown in Table 3-1 applies to this simple bus circuit.

When none of the buffers has been enabled or connected to the bus, the bus is not connected to anything except the input of the gates, memories, etc., that are the "receivers" of the data bit, so the

Table 3-1. Truth Table for a Four-Device Three-State Bus

| Enable | | | | Bus Content |
|---|---|---|---|---|
| D | C | B | A | |
| 1 | 1 | 1 | 1 | Undetermined (all devices HI-Z) |
| 1 | 1 | 1 | 0 | Data A |
| 1 | 1 | 0 | 1 | Data B |
| 1 | 0 | 1 | 1 | Data C |
| 0 | 1 | 1 | 1 | Data D |
| 0 | 0 | 0 | 0 | Not Allowed |

logic value of the bus is unknown. Whenever a logic zero is applied to one of the bus buffer enable inputs, *the selected buffer* passes its data onto the bus. The condition in which more than one buffer has been enabled is not allowed, since bus conflicts will arise.

All of the devices that are to be used with the Apple computer system to transfer information to the CPU *must* have three-state outputs. Thus, even memory chips must have three-state outputs, as they in fact do. The computer designer must be sure that the system has been designed so that no two input devices are selected at the same time. If such a multiple selection takes place, improper operation of the computer occurs.

Input ports that may be used to transfer information to the computer are readily constructed using standard three-state integrated circuits. In most cases, eight individual three-state buffers are used, one per bus line. In most cases, too, the enable inputs are all connected in parallel, so that all eight buffers transfer their information onto the bus simultaneously. In some cases, the common enabling input is provided within the chip so that only a single pin on the chip is required for the control of all eight bits.

There are many chips that may be used to construct input ports, but only a few of them are general enough to warrant our consideration. The two main integrated circuits that will be used in our examples are the SN74365 and the SN74LS244. The SN74365 may also be noted as the DM8095 (National Semiconductor Corp.), which is an exact replacement. The pin configuration for these two chips is shown in Fig. 3-9.

You will note quickly that while the SN74LS244 has eight three-state buffers on one chip, the SN74365 has only six. If the SN74365 device is used to construct an input port, two of the integrated circuit packages must be used. A typical 8-bit input port is shown in Fig. 3-10. In this case, only two of the three-state buffers in the lower SN74365 chip have been used. Since the SN74365 contains built-in

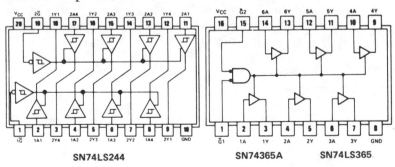

SN74LS244                SN74365A        SN74LS365

Fig. 3-9. SN74LS244 and SN74365 (DM8095) three-state bus driver chip
pin configuration.

NOR gates that control the enabling of the three-state buffers, these have been used to gate the $\overline{RD}$ function pulse and the device address, $\overline{49321}$. If the device select signal, $\overline{RD\ 49321}$, had already been generated elsewhere in the interface circuit, it could be applied to one of the enable inputs on both chips, while the other enable inputs were grounded, or logic zero. This control scheme is shown in Fig. 3-11.

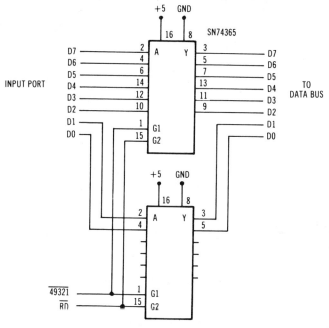

Fig. 3-10. Typical input port constructed using SN74365 chips.

Using such an input port, data values may be input to the computer through the use of the PEEK command, as shown in Example 3-2.

**Example 3-2. Data Input Program for Port 49321**

```
10   A = PEEK (49321)
20   PRINT A
30   GOTO 10
```

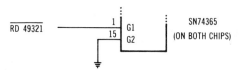

Fig. 3-11. Alternate control scheme for SN74365 three-state chips.

In this example, the 8-bit binary value is converted to a decimal number between zero and 255 when it is input by the Apple using the PEEK command at line 10 in the program. It is then "printed" on the video monitor screen. It would have been just as valid to use the following command:

```
10  PRINT PEEK(49321): GOTO 10
```

A similar input port may be constructed by using an SN74LS244 octal (8-bit) buffer. This chip contains two independent sets of four buffers each, which are independently controlled with two enable inputs, $\overline{2G}$ and $\overline{1G}$. Since there are no built-in NOR gates in the SN74-LS244, external device select gating is required. A typical input port in which an SN74LS244 chip has been used is shown in Fig. 3-12. Software steps similar to those shown in Example 3-2 would be used

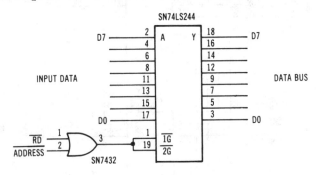

Fig. 3-12. Input port configured with an SN74LS244 chip.

to control the flow of information from this port into the computer.

Both the SN74365 and the SN74LS244 have pin-for-pin equivalent circuits that *invert the data bits* as they are passed through the chips and onto the data bus. These buffers are the SN74366 and the SN74LS240, respectively. The SN74366 is also equivalent to the DN8096 chip. In most cases, the noninverting buffers will be the ones used in interface circuits.

In some cases, peripheral devices may generate more than eight bits of information that must be read by the computer. An example of such a device would be a 12-bit analog-to-digital converter. When more than eight bits of information are to be input, the bits are divided into groups of eight bits. In the case of the 12-bit converter, there would be two groups, one containing 8 bits, and the other containing the remaining four bits. Likewise, a 16-bit value would require two input ports, as would a 9-bit value. When not all eight bits in an input port are used, the unused bits are generally placed in the logic zero state by connecting them to ground, or logic zero. If the state of the unused bits cannot be determined, perhaps they have not actually been constructed in the input port circuit. You can "eliminate" these bits by using appropriate software commands. These commands "mask" these unused bits, so that they become zeros.

Since a 12-bit value may represent decimal values between 0 and 4095, some means must be found for converting the individual bytes that have been input into a single value. We will assume that the eight least-significant bits have been input as a single byte from port 49312, and that the four most-significant bits have been input from input port 49313 at bit positions D3-D0. We will further assume that the unused bits at input port 49313 have been grounded so that they are logic zeros.

Now that the configuration of the input ports has been defined, let's see how the information is manipulated so that the original value is reconstructed from the two separate bytes of data from the two input ports (Fig. 3-13). Since the least-significant bits can represent values between 0 and 255 from the 12-bit interface device, these bits do not require any "conversion," since the Apple will simply input

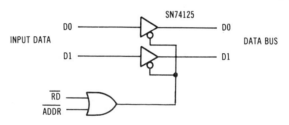

Fig. 3-13. Two-bit input port.

these eight bits and convert them to a value within the range of 0 to 255. However, if the four most-significant bits are considered apart from the other bits, converting them to decimal will yield values between 0 and 15, rather than their original positional values of 0, 256, 512, and so on. These bits have been "offset" by a factor of 256 due to the fact that the 12-bit data value had to be "split" into smaller pieces so that it could be input by the Apple. Remember that any 8-bit value that is input into the Apple will be automatically converted into a decimal number with values in the range of 0 to 255.

When the two values have been input into the Apple, it is a simple matter to "reconstruct" the data. If the information from the four most-significant bits is multiplied by 256 and then added to the value from the eight least-significant bits, a resulting value will represent values between 0 and 4095, inclusive, the value that was originally present as a 12-bit binary value at the interface device. The complete software routine is shown in Example 3-3.

**Example 3-3. Program for a 12-Bit Input Conversion**

```
10   A  =  PEEK(49312)
20   B  =  PEEK(49313)
30   C  =  (B  *  256)  +  A
40   PRINT C
```

You could simplify this by placing all of the steps on one line:

```
10   PRINT(PEEK(49313)  *  256)  +  PEEK(49312)
```

This simple program will print the decimal equivalent of the 12-bit binary value that was present at the peripheral or interface device when the program was run. The program can be used for interfaces with from 9 to 16 binary outputs, but you must be careful to ground the unused bits. You will see another method of "masking," or clearing the bits in the experiments.

Input ports are used to transfer information from external devices to the computer. This information may represent actual values of weight, temperature, resistance, etc., or the information may be interpreted as individual binary bits representing the state (on or off) of individual devices, for example, empty/full, ready/busy, etc. Some typical uses for input ports would include the following:

Transfer of traffic sensor information to the computer
Transfer of digital values from an instrument to the computer
Transfer of status (on-off) bits from a printer to the computer

In interfacing applications, the main requirement for input ports is that their outputs have three states so that they will not cause conflicts on the data bus when they are used.

# CHAPTER 4

# Flags and Decisions

In almost all of the previous examples, we have assumed that there is little synchronization required between the computer and the external I/O devices. Thus, output ports have been assumed to always be ready for more data to be transferred to them. In the case of input ports, we have assumed that the data values are present and ready for transfer to the computer, when the computer reaches a PEEK command in a program. This may not always be the case. We must often deal with I/O devices that are slower than the computer.

## I/O DEVICE SYNCHRONIZATION

Since not all I/O devices may be ready for the computer at all times, a means of synchronizing the computer and the I/O devices is required. The synchronization generally involves the use of signals that are called *flags*. These signals are used to indicate that various devices are busy or not busy, ready or not ready, converting or not converting, and so on. Thus, "flags" indicate the status of devices, and they are often called *status flags*.

For illustrative purposes, we will assume that we are required to interface a device to an Apple computer. The device will provide 8-bit data values to the computer on an irregular basis. In most cases, such devices also generate a flag signal that indicates that the device is ready to transfer its information to the computer. Such a device is shown in Fig. 4-1. Note that a standard three-state input port has been used to transfer the information to the computer. The READY flag presents an interesting problem. How is the computer going to monitor or check the condition of the READY flag, so that it can determine when a new data value is ready?

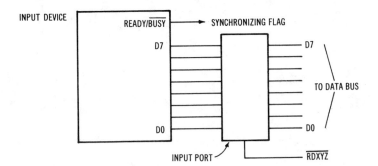

Fig. 4-1. Simple input device with synchronizing flag output.

As we stated previously, there is no rule that limits input ports to the transfer of actual numeric values. The computer has no way of knowing that the 8-bit value, $01100100_2$, represents 100, rather than five devices being off, and three devices being on. Thus, another input port could serve quite well as a way of transferring the status flag information from the input device to the computer. The other seven bits at this input port may be unused, or they may be used to indicate the status of other external devices. In this way, software steps may be used to check the condition or status of external devices.

When the status of a flag is checked in a computer program, the computer may be programmed to wait until a flag has changed to a particular state before going on with the required action, or it may be programmed to check the flag periodically, going on about other tasks in the meantime.

There are logic operations in assembly language and in BASIC that allow us to check the status of individual flags, or bits, in an 8-bit data word. In this way, the actual logic zero or logic one state of a flag may be detected, with the computer making a decision based upon the state of the flag.

## LOGICAL OPERATIONS AND FLAGS

Probably the most useful operation, where flag detection is concerned, is the logic AND operation. You should recall that two bits, A and B, may be "ANDed" together, as shown in Fig. 4-2. The result indicates that only when both of the bits are logic ones will the result be a logic one. Another way to think of this is to treat the "A" bit as

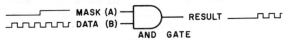

Fig. 4-2. Representation of logical AND operation using DATA and MASK to yield RESULT.

| VALUE | 00111010 | 00011010 | 11110000 | 00011111 |
|---|---|---|---|---|
| MASK | 00100000 | 00100000 | 00100000 | 00100000 |
| RESULT | 00100000 | 00000000 | 00100000 | 00000000 |

Fig. 4-3. Example of AND operation in which eight bits of information are operated on.

a "mask," and the "B" bit as information or data. When the mask is a zero, the result is a zero. When the mask is a one, the data is passed through the gate. In this way, selected bits may be masked, while others are "passed through" the mask. If, for example, we wished to check the state of bit D5 in the data word 00111010, a mask of 00100000 could be used. The mask is ANDed with the data word, as shown in Fig. 4-3, for several different data words. In all cases, the logic state of D5 was passed through to bit D5 in the result. All of the other bits were masked, or set to zero. In this way, the total result was zero when bit D5 was zero, and the result was nonzero when bit D5 was a one. This could be used as the basis for decision making steps in a program. You must remember to convert the masks to their decimal equivalent before trying to use them in a BASIC program. In the case of bit D5, the mask would be converted to 32.

## FLAG-DETECTING SOFTWARE

Once an interface has been constructed so that the states of the various flags may be detected, as shown in Fig. 4-4, software may be used to make decisions based upon the states of the flags.

In some dialects of BASIC, there are logical operations that will perform bit-by-bit AND operations, such as the ones shown in Fig. 4-3. In these cases, simple expressions may be used in BASIC pro-

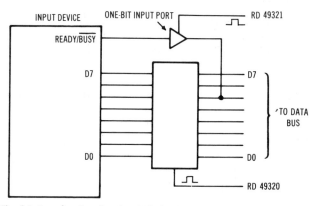

Fig. 4-4. Complete interface in which the flag is detected by software.

### Example 4-1. A Logic Zero Used for Control

```
4010   A = PEEK(49321)
4020   IF (A AND 32) = 0 THEN 200
4030   . . . Continue here if flag = logic one
```

grams to perform the ANDing operations between two data words that have values between 0 and 255. Keep in mind that the *binary equivalents* are what is actually being ANDed. Examples 4-1 and 4-2 illustrate how these AND operations could be used to detect a flag that is input at bit D5 from an input port, port 49321.

### Example 4-2. A Logic One Flag Used for Control

```
4010   A = PEEK(49321)
4020   IF (A AND 32) > 0 THEN 200
4030   . . . Continue here if flag = logic zero
```

In either case, when the proper condition is met, the program would probably input data from an input port, or perform some other action that is signaled by the presence of the flag.

Unfortunately, the Apple computer does not use its logical commands in this way. In the Apple, an AND operation allows only the ANDing of two distinct true-or-false conditions, so it is very difficult to mask eight bits to determine the state on only one. Unless we wish to spend a great deal of time in a complex BASIC routine, we must consider the use of an assembly-language subroutine that will perform the logical operations for us rather quickly. Since you can easily point the Apple to assembly-language routines, this is worth pursuing a bit further. In fact, we will provide you with some simple, easy-to-use routines.

## ASSEMBLY-LANGUAGE LOGICAL OPERATIONS

The assembly-language instruction set for the 6502 microprocessor contains an AND and an OR operation. Each of these instructions will operate upon two 8-bit bytes, providing a single byte as the result of the operation. Thus, we must write a short routine that will perform the operation.

The Apple provides some "spare" read/write memory locations on memory page 03H, and we have chosen to locate our routines on this page, since it will make the routines independent of the total memory size of your computer. A complete listing for the routine is provided in Table 4-1. Note that both hexadecimal and decimal addresses and data/instruction values are provided for you. You do not have to be an expert in assembly language programming to use this routine, but we have provided some comments so that you can follow the operation of the program, if you wish.

Table 4-1. Assembly-Language Logic Subroutine

| Address Byte | | Data Byte | | |
|---|---|---|---|---|
| Hexadecimal | Decimal | Hexadecimal | Decimal | |
| 0300 | 768 | — | — | MASK Byte Goes Here |
| 0301 | 769 | — | — | DATA Byte Goes Here |
| 0302 | 770 | — | — | ANSWER Found Here |
| 0303 | 771 | 48 | 72 | PHA Push Reg A |
| 0304 | 772 | AD | 173 | LDA Load Reg A from |
| 0305 | 773 | 00 | 0 | MASK location |
| 0306 | 774 | 03 | 3 | |
| 0307 | 775 | 2D | 45 | AND Reg A with DATA * |
| 0308 | 776 | 01 | 1 | |
| 0309 | 777 | 03 | 3 | |
| 030A | 778 | 8D | 141 | STA Store result in |
| 030B | 779 | 02 | 2 | ANSWER location |
| 030C | 780 | 03 | 3 | |
| 030D | 781 | 68 | 104 | PLA Pull Reg A back |
| 030E | 782 | 60 | 96 | RTS Return to BASIC |

*Substitute 0DH, or 13 decimal, for an OR operation.

Three read/write memory locations are used for the temporary storage of the various data bytes, called MASK, BYTE, and AN-SWER. The MASK location is loaded with the mask byte, and the BYTE location is loaded with the byte that is to be operated on. After the logical operation has taken place, the ANSWER location contains the result.

To use this routine, you need to load the MASK information into address 768, and the DATA byte into address 769. You can use POKE operations to do this. Once this is done, you simply need to call the assembly-language subroutine, so that the operation is performed. How do you do this?

Calling an assembly-language subroutine from BASIC is not very difficult. In the Apple computer, you simply need to put a three-byte jump instruction in three successive locations, addresses 10, 11, and 12, or 0A, 0B, and 0C, in hexadecimal notation. Since our routine starts at address 771, or 0303H, you need to put the following information in these three locations: a 76 in address 10, a 3 in address 11, and a 3 in address 12. Once you have loaded this address information into these three locations, you can access the assembly-language subroutine with a USR function. In this case, you need to first load the MASK and BYTE information, and *then* use the USR function. This is shown in Example 4-3.

In this case, the value 32 is the mask byte, and 129 is the value that is to be ANDed with it. The Q is a "dummy" variable that is required for the use of the USR function, and the value 5 is a "dummy" value that has no effect on the subroutine. You can use any variable for Q,

Example 4-3. Calling the Logical Operation Subroutine

```
1590   POKE 768,32: POKE 769,129
1594   Q  =  USR(5)
```

as long as you don't use it elsewhere, and you may substitute any value for the 5, say 0.

Once you have called the assembly-language subroutine, you will find the result in location 770, and a PEEK operation may be used to get at it. The program shown in Example 4-4 shows the complete use of the subroutine. We have assumed that the subroutine has been loaded, probably through the use of the monitor. In this example, the three-byte jump instruction is loaded by using POKE operations.

**Example 4-4. Using the Logic Operation Subroutine**

```
2030   POKE 10,76: POKE 11,3: POKE 12,3
2040   POKE 768,32: POKE 769,PEEK(49321)
2050   Q  =  USR(7)
2060   IF PEEK(770) > 0 THEN 3460
2070   . . . Continue here if flag = 0
```

In this example, the data to be used in the logical operation is obtained from an input port by using a PEEK command and the address for the device.

You can also perform an OR operation with the same subroutine, simply by changing the operation code (op-code) for the AND operation from a 2DH to a 0DH. Again, a POKE operation can do this just before you use the subroutine. Thus, the subroutine provided in Table 4-1 can be used for both logical operations.

You should be able to load the subroutine into the read/write memory by using the monitor for the Apple. We refer you to the *Apple II Reference Manual* for information about the monitor. You could also use 12 POKE commands to load the program steps, but this invites errors.

It is unfortunate that you must resort to assembly language to perform the logical operations that are readily available in other BASIC dialects. However, the assembly-language program is fairly simple, and it has provided a simple example of the use of such programs, and how they can be called from a BASIC program. If you are not an assembly-language programmer, perhaps this has whetted your appetite.

## COMPLEX FLAGS

At this point, you may be asking, if the flag on the input device shown in Fig. 4-4 is used to indicate the availability of an 8-bit value, how does the device know when the computer has input, or ac-

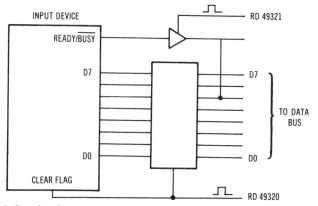

Fig. 4-5. Complete flag circuit in which flag is cleared by computer-generated pulse.

cepted, the value that it has made available? In some cases, a signal from the computer to the I/O device is used to indicate that the flag has been detected, and that the necessary action has taken place. This signal "clears" the flag. The flag-clearing action may be performed by a separate signal. The same signal that controls the input port for the data may perform the flag-clearing action. This is shown in Fig. 4-5, and a simple timing diagram is shown in Fig. 4-6.

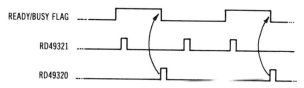

Fig. 4-6. Flag timing diagram.

When the flag is placed in the logic one state, this indicates that the device is ready to transfer a byte to the computer. The RD 49321 pulse represents the transfer of the flag status information to the computer. When the computer tests the flag and finds that it is a logic one, it executes the steps that actually transfer the data from the device to the computer. The RD 49320 pulse is used here to enable the three-state buffers at the correct time. This pulse is also used to clear the internal flag circuit of the device.

The second RD 49321 pulse again reads the status of the flag, but since the flag is now a logic zero, the computer takes no further action. The third time that the flag is tested, however, the flag is a logic one, and the data is transferred to the computer and the flag is cleared. A simple set of program steps that can be used to control the interface is provided in Example 4-5. We have assumed that the logical AND subroutine has been loaded, along with the three-byte pointer.

Example 4-5. A Simple Flag Testing Program

```
1050  POKE 768,32: POKE 769,PEEK(49321)
1060  Q = USR(0)
1070  IF PEEK(770) = 0 THEN 50
1080  D = PEEK(49320)
1090  . . . Continue here after data input
```

Typical devices that use flags in this way are keyboards, floppy disks, analog-to-digital converters, and other devices that may provide data bytes at irregular periods.

## FLAG CIRCUITS

In some cases, devices may not have the necessary flag circuits within them for easy flag control, or they may not generate logic levels that are stable for relatively "long" periods so that they can be properly detected by the computer. In these cases, the "flag" may be a very short pulse. In fact, some flag pulses are too short to be detected by the computer, if they are simply input by means of a three-state input port.

In cases such as this, it is necessary to design a circuit that will "capture" the flag pulse so that it may be detected by the computer sometime later. Even if the computer can test a flag bit every few milliseconds, it will frequently "miss" short pulses of a few microseconds duration.

Flip-flop or latch circuits are generally used to remember the presence of flag pulses. Typical flip-flop devices are the SN7474 D-type flip-flop, and the SN7476 J-K flip-flop. Most introductory digital electronics books provide a good coverage of flip-flop devices if you need to review their operation.

A typical flip-flop-based flag circuit is shown in Fig. 4-7. In this circuit, the input device generates a READY pulse that *clocks* the flip-flop, transferring the logic level from the D input to the Q output. The Q output is detected by the computer through the use of an input port that is separate from the input port that is used for the transfer of the eight data bits. The status of the flag bit is easily tested by the computer, as has been described. Once the necessary action has taken place, in this case, the input of data from the input device, the flag flip-flop is cleared. A logic zero pulse, CLEAR, applied to the clear input of the flip-flop serves this purpose. While the RD 49360 pulse used to control the 8-bit input port could be used to clear the flip-flop, we have shown a separate clear signal, so that the timing relationships can be shown, as in Fig. 4-8.

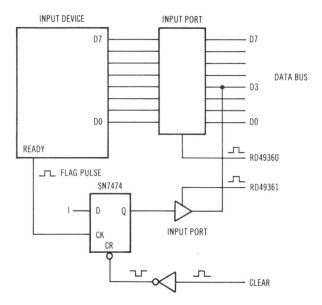

Fig. 4-7. Flip-flop circuit used for detection of flag pulse.

In the timing diagram, the READY pulse sets the flip-flop, so that its Q output is a logic one. This is detected when the status flag information is input from port 49361. The logic one state of the flag causes the software to perform the steps that input the data byte and then clear the flag. The separate CLEAR signal could be generated by a POKE command, and appropriate circuitry, although the use of the readily available RD 40360 pulse is probably easier.

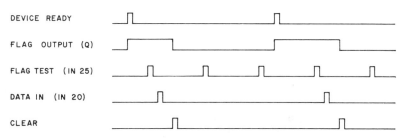

Fig. 4-8. Flag flip-flop timing diagram.

In this example, the flag was tested twice while it was in the logic zero state. Since this indicated that no new data was ready, no input transfers or flag clears were initiated.

Several experiments at the end of this book involve the use of flags.

## MULTIPLE FLAGS

Many systems have a number of flags that must be checked on a regular basis. In some cases, a priority must be established, since some devices are more important, or require faster attention, than do others. The priority is easily set in the program, since the order in which the various bits are tested determines which devices are "serviced" before others. The program steps shown in Example 4-6 will check several flag bits in sequence, from bit D7 to bit D5, providing a priority in the order in which the corresponding devices would be serviced by the computer.

In this example, the flag for bit D7 was detected when it was a logic one, while the other two flags were detected when they were logic zero. Other bit-sensing steps may be added for other flags, and the order in which the bits are tested may be changed at any time, simply by changing the program to reflect the new order. Note that the data involved in the AND operation is not changed, and it only needs to be input from the input port at the start of the sequence of instructions.

**Example 4-6. Flag Priority Software Steps**

```
300   POKE 769,PEEK(54098):POKE 768,128: Q=USR(0)
305   IF PEEK(770) > 0 THEN 1050
310   POKE 768,64:Q=USR(0)
315   IF PEEK(770) = 0 THEN 20
320   POKE 768,32:Q=USR(0)
325   IF PEEK(770) = 0 THEN 1010
330   . . . And so on for other bits
```

## INTERRUPTS

In some cases, it is necessary for an I/O device to be serviced as soon as it is ready. It may not be able to wait the many milliseconds, or even longer periods, that the computer may require to check flags and make decisions based upon them. Almost all computers have at least one interrupt input that allows you to "demand" immediate servicing from the computer, irrespective of what it is doing. The 6502 processor chip used in the Apple computer has two interrupt inputs; an interrupt request input (IRQ), and a nonmaskable interrupt input (NMI). The IRQ input is sensitive to a logic zero, while the NMI input is *edge sensitive*, being triggered by a logic one to logic zero transition. These inputs are not used within the basic Apple computer. However, they are readily available at the internal interface connectors, and they may be used by add-on peripheral devices and interfaces.

If a device is going to require extremely fast servicing, fast enough to require the use of an interrupt, it goes without saying that assembly-language programming will also be required. Since this is beyond the scope of this book, we refer you to *Programming & Interfacing the 6502, With Experiments* and *6502 Software Design*, Howard W. Sams & Co., Inc., Indianapolis, IN 46268. Both books discuss the use of interrupts in detail, providing examples and assembly-language programs for the control of interrupts.

The Apple interrupts IRQ and NMI use specific memory locations from which the 6502 processor "fetches" the address of the subroutine that is to be used as the service routine for each interrupt. The IRQ uses locations FFFEH and FFFFH, and the NMI uses locations FFFAH and FFFBH. Since these locations are actually within the read-only memory chips that contain the BASIC interpreter and the monitor, the addresses in these four locations are fixed and you cannot change them. However, these fixed addresses are simply used to point to other locations in read/write memory where you can actually change the pointers for the interrupt service subroutines. We refer you to the *Apple II Reference Manual* for the details of how to use these "vector" locations.

### FINAL WORDS

A few final words are necessary before you leave this chapter. We have chosen to introduce you to a simple assembly-language subroutine for performing the logical AND or OR manipulation on two 8-bit bytes, along with the use of the assembly-language subroutine calling operation, USR. Actually, the Apple computer has a flag-checking command in its instruction set: WAIT. This instruction can be used to check individual flags, or groups of flags, and it can detect logic one and logic zero flags, too. However, there is a limitation to its use. If the proper flag pattern is not detected, then there is no way for you to ever leave the flag-checking operation, and you must *reset* the computer to get back control. Likewise, you cannot decide to branch to one portion of a program if the flag or flags are set, and to branch in another direction if they are not set. If the WAIT command is used, you will simply continue to WAIT until the condition is met. This is fairly inflexible, and we have chosen to avoid the use of the WAIT command for this purpose.

We have introduced you to the USR command for calling assembly-language subroutines, and if you expand your horizons and continue to learn more about assembly-language programming, you will find that this instruction is quite valuable. However, if you simply want to access an assembly-language subroutine, such as the logical AND subroutine, you can use the CALL command, followed by the *decimal* address of the start of the subroutine. A CALL 771 operation can be used to call the logical AND subroutine. Of course, you must POKE the MASK and DATA bytes before you call the subroutine.

The object here has been to show you a bit more of the power of the Apple computer and how it can handle different tasks. The easy path isn't often the most interesting or educational.

# CHAPTER 5

# Breadboarding
# with the Apple

It has always been our philosophy that computers should be easy to use, both for program development and for hardware or interface development. Since the necessary signals for interfacing most computers are readily available somewhere in the computer system, it was decided to develop some general-purpose interface circuits that could be used with a number of different computers. These circuits are fairly simple and are easily constructed and adapted to many computers besides the Apple. A printed circuit was developed containing all of the necessary circuits for interfacing purposes. A photograph of the interface is shown in Fig. 5-1. A standard 40-conductor flat cable is used to connect the interface breadboard to various computers. While the interfacing circuits could have been breadboarded and then used for the experiments, it was thought that this would only provide additional points at which problems could surface.

## BASIC BREADBOARD

The basic breadboard contains a number of useful circuits that allow interface designs to be easily set up and tested. The basic sections are Power Supply, Logic Probe, Device and Memory Decoders, Bus Buffers, and Control Circuitry.

### Power Supply

The power supply section of the breadboard may be operated in one of two ways. An external +5-volt power supply may be used, as

Fig. 5-1. Apple breadboard system.

long as it can supply 1 ampere of current, or an external transformer may be used to supply 12.6 volts (ac) to the on-board power supply circuits. In either case, the breadboard power supply is separate from the computer power supply. A separate power supply is often used because some computer systems cannot supply sufficient power for their own circuits *and* the added interface circuits that you may wish to test. Whenever an external power supply is used, *you must be sure that there is a good, low-resistance common ground connection between both power supplies.* A power supply schematic is shown in Fig. 5-2.

If the on-board power supply is to be used, the 12.6-V ac transformer is connected to pins 1 and 2 on plug number 1 (P1); the rectifier diodes, D1-D4, the filter capacitor, C1, and the voltage regulator, VR, are all installed. We suggest that a small heat sink be used with the +5-volt regulator. When the breadboard is used in this manner, +5 volts are available at pin 5, and ground is available at pin 6, on P1. These connections may be used for external devices, if required.

If a separate +5-volt power supply is to be used, the power supply parts D1-D4, C1, and VR are not needed and should be removed or not installed. The +5-volt and ground connections are made at pins 5 and 6, respectively, at P1.

Since other voltages are often required, such as ±12 or ±15 volts, provision has been made at P1 to connect additional external power

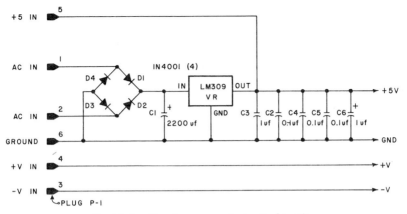

Fig. 5-2. Breadboard power-supply circuit schematic.

supplies. The positive voltage, +V, and negative voltage, −V, are connected to pins 4 and 3, respectively, at P1.

All of the voltages are available at the socket at position IC-16. The available connections are shown in Table 5-1.

Table 5-1. Power Supply Connections for the Power Socket, IC-16

| Pin* | Voltage Available |
|---|---|
| 7,10 | +5 |
| 5,12 | GND |
| 3,14 | +V (External) |
| 1,16 | −V (External) |

*All other pins are unconnected.

Power for the integrated circuits on the printed-circuit board has been derived from the +5-volt power supply. The connections at IC-16 (socket) provide a means of easily obtaining power for the experiments.

### Logic Probe

The logic probe circuit, Fig. 5-3, is useful in determining the logic state of various outputs, and also for detecting pulse activity at outputs. The logic-probe section of the breadboard contains a level detector and a pulse detector circuit. An LM-319 (IC-15) comparator has been used to detect the logic one and logic zero levels, while an SN74LS123 (IC-14) has been used to detect and "stretch" pulses. We have used a green light-emitting diode (LED) for the logic zero indicator (D-7), a red LED for the logic one indicator (D-6) and a yellow LED for the pulse indicator (D-5). The input to the probe is available at pins 1-4 at IC socket IC-19. These inputs are marked

"P." All of these inputs are in parallel, and any one may be used, but do not try and connect the logic probe to two signals at the same time. The logic probe should be thought of as two low-power Schottky (LS) input loads.

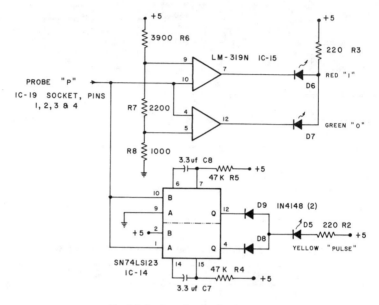

Fig. 5-3. Logic probe circuit schematic.

If you have an external logic probe, the circuitry in this section may not be needed. If you wish, you do not have to construct this portion of the circuit. In any case, it will be useful to be able to detect pulses and also to be able to detect the state of pulses, etc. We have found the logic probe to be very useful in troubleshooting breadboarded interface circuits.

## Memory and Device Decoders

A major portion of the circuitry on the breadboard is devoted to I/O address decoding, as shown in Fig. 5-4. The decoders can be operated in either a device mode or a memory mode, depending upon the type of computer in use. In device addressing, only the LO address bits (A7-A0) are decoded, while in memory addressing, all of the address bits (A15-A0) are decoded. The Apple computer uses memory addressing to identify I/O devices, since it is based upon the 6502 microprocessor chip. Likewise, computers based upon the 6800 microprocessor also use memory addressing. Computers built around the 8080, 8085, and Z-80 family of chips can use either type

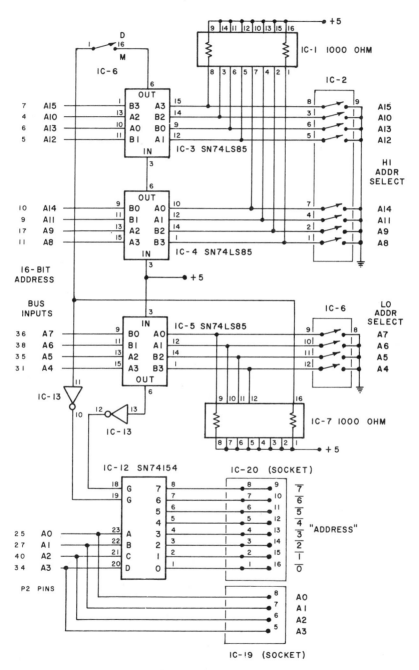

Fig. 5-4. Address decoder circuit schematic.

73

of addressing. As you look over the schematic in Fig. 5-4, you should recognize that the address decoding uses a combination of digital comparators and decoders.

In the device addressing mode, an SN74LS85 4-bit comparator (IC-5) is used to compare preset address bits to the address bits present on the LO address bus lines A7-A4. The switches at IC-6 are used to preset the logic levels that will be compared with the address bus. The package at IC-6 is a set of dual-in-line switches, so care is required in making the switch settings. The switch positions are clearly marked, "7," "6," "5," and "4" at the switch marked "LO." If you are installing the switch, be sure that the open or off position is to the right (logic one position). Pull-up resistors at IC-7 provide the logic one inputs to the SN74LS85 when the switches are open, or in the logic one position.

When an address match occurs between the preset bits and address bits A7-A4, the SN74154 decoder (IC-12) is enabled. Although the SN74154 decoder has the ability to decode address bits A3-A0 into 16 unique address outputs, only the first 8 have been used, more than enough for breadboarding and interface testing.

Thus, if the address switches for bits 7-4 are set to 1011, the decoder would decode addresses $10110000_2$ through $10110111_2$, or addresses 176 through 183, decimal. For device addressing, the lowest switch at IC-6 must be "open" or in the "D" position. This places the decoder in the correct mode.

The decoded-address outputs are present at the IC-20 socket. They are labeled "0," "1," and so on, through "7." The entire section is called "ADDRESS." Note that there is a bar over the address numbers to indicate that the unique output state is a logic zero pulse. The address notation, zero through seven, is a sequential addressing that will help you in determining which pins are connected to the device address outputs. *In most cases, the numbers will have no relationship to the actual addresses that have been decoded.* In the addressing example cited previously, in which addresses 176 through 183 were decoded, the output labeled "0" would correspond to the decoded address of 176. Table 5-2 details the decoder outputs that are available at the address socket, IC-20.

Memory addresses are also easy to decode on the interface breadboard. Two additional comparator chips, IC-3 and IC-4, are used to compare address-bus lines A15-A8 with a preset HI address. The HI address bits are set at the eight-switch dual-in-line package of switches labeled HI, at IC-2. When using memory addressing, you must be careful not to try and select addresses that have been assigned to the internal Apple memory (ROM or R/W). You must also remember to convert the complete 16-bit address into the equivalent decimal value for use in PEEK and POKE instructions.

In the memory address mode, you must place the lowest switch at IC-6 in the "closed" or in the "M" position. This allows the SN74154 decoder to be activated only when there is a match between address bits A15-A8 and the bits preset at the HI dip-switch *and* a match between address bits A7-A4 and the bits preset at the LO dip-switch. Thus, addresses between XXXXXXXX XXXX0000 and XXXXXXXX XXXX0111 are accessible, where X=1 or 0. These decoded addresses are present as logic zero pulses at the "ADDRESS" socket (IC-20). Remember that only the first eight addresses in a selected 16-address block are available. Thus, if 10000001 is set for the HI address and 1110 is set for the LO address (bits A7-A4), addresses 33248 through 33256 would generate logic zero pulses at pins 1 through 8 at the "ADDRESS" socket, respectively. Keep in mind that the SN74154 decoder decodes all 16 addresses; you only have access to the "lower" eight.

**Table 5-2. Address-Decoder Connections for the Address Socket, IC-20**

| Pin (IC-20) | Designation | SN74154 Output Pin |
|:---:|:---:|:---:|
| 1,16 | 0 | 1 |
| 2,15 | 1 | 2 |
| 3,14 | 2 | 3 |
| 4,13 | 3 | 4 |
| 5,12 | 4 | 5 |
| 6,11 | 5 | 6 |
| 7,10 | 6 | 7 |
| 8,9 | 7 | 8 |

Connections for address-bus lines A3-A0 (unbuffered) are available on the breadboard at pins 8-5, respectively, on the socket at IC-19. These signals may be used in some experiments, but caution is required, since these signals are not buffered, and present a direct connection to the Apple computer.

The address decoder section of the breadboard will save you a great deal of time and effort, because you will not have to construct device address decoder circuits when you wish to implement I/O ports, or try some simple interface circuits.

**Bus Buffers**

Two 8216 noninverting bus buffer chips, IC-10 and IC-11, have been used to buffer the bus, as shown in Fig. 5-5. This means that the bus is available with a full fan-out of 30 (it can power 30 standard 7400-type inputs) and that it is isolated from the Apple data bus. The eight bits on the data bus are available at the socket at IC-18.

The information in Table 5-3 shows the connections to the data bus.

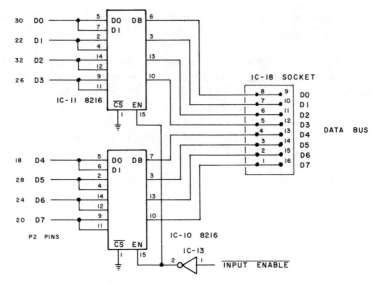

Fig. 5-5. Bus buffer circuit schematic.

The bus buffers are always enabled, and the normal mode of operation is for the transfer of data *from the Apple to the breadboard*. This means that without additional signal use, you could monitor the bus "activity" by connecting logic probes or other suitable monitors to the outputs of the bus buffer chips, D7-D0. Output ports are implemented by simply using the proper control signals (described in the next section) to control an 8-bit latch. The eight latch inputs are connected to D7-D0 at the socket IC-18.

Input ports, however, must be implemented so that they turn the bus buffers in the opposite direction to "drive" data into the Apple. Actually, there are two bus buffers for each bus line, as shown in the pin configuration shown in Fig. 5-6 for the 8216 buffer. The DIEN input determines which set of buffers is enabled, thus directing data to, or from, the Apple. All input operations must activate the proper

Table 5-3. Data Bus Connections at IC-18

| Pin (IC-18) | Data Bus Signal |
|---|---|
| 1,16 | D7 |
| 2,15 | D6 |
| 3,14 | D5 |
| 4,13 | D4 |
| 5,12 | D3 |
| 6,11 | D2 |
| 7,10 | D1 |
| 8,9 | D0 |

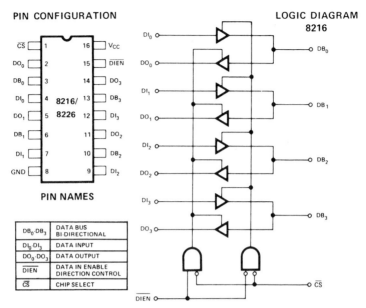

## PIN CONFIGURATION

| | | | |
|---|---|---|---|
| $\overline{CS}$ | 1 | 16 | $V_{CC}$ |
| $DO_0$ | 2 | 15 | $\overline{DIEN}$ |
| $DB_0$ | 3 | 14 | $DO_3$ |
| $DI_0$ | 4 | 13 | $DB_3$ |
| $DO_1$ | 5 | 12 | $DI_3$ |
| $DB_1$ | 6 | 11 | $DO_2$ |
| $DI_1$ | 7 | 10 | $DB_2$ |
| GND | 8 | 9 | $DI_2$ |

8216/ 8226

## LOGIC DIAGRAM
### 8216

## PIN NAMES

| | |
|---|---|
| $DB_0$-$DB_3$ | DATA BUS BI-DIRECTIONAL |
| $DI_0$-$DI_3$ | DATA INPUT |
| $DO_0$-$DO_3$ | DATA OUTPUT |
| $\overline{DIEN}$ | DATA IN ENABLE DIRECTION CONTROL |
| $\overline{CS}$ | CHIP SELECT |

**Fig. 5-6. The 8216 bus buffer chip pin configuration.**

set of buffers so that the Apple receives the data properly. Special control circuitry has been provided to do this for input operations.

### Control Circuitry

The control circuitry on the breadboard is rather simple, consisting mainly of some general-purpose buffers to buffer control signals output by the computer. Six signals are provided, $\overline{IN}$, $\overline{RD}$, $\overline{OUT}$, $\overline{WR}$, $\overline{RESET}$, and $\overline{INTAK}$. For Apple interfacing, you will only be concerned with the $\overline{WR}$, $\overline{RD}$, and $\overline{RESET}$ signals. The other signals are useful when the breadboard is used with other computers. This control circuitry is shown in Fig. 5-7. The general-purpose interrupt signal is also buffered, but it is an input to the computer. Connections to the control signals are made at the socket at IC-17, as noted in Table 5-4.

The control circuitry also generates a signal that switches the 8216 bus buffers into the input mode, so that data may be transferred into the Apple. It would seem to be merely a matter of turning the bus around whenever a memory read operation took place. If this were implemented, the bus buffers on the breadboard would be placed in the input mode, even when a memory chip was activated within the Apple. This would cause a bus "conflict," so the bus on the breadboard must be placed in the input mode only when an input device on the breadboard itself has been selected.

To handle input ports properly, the input port device select signal is used to gate data onto the data bus and also to control the mode of the 8216 bus buffers. In effect, up to four input port device select pulses may be ORed together to place the breadboard bus buffers in the input mode. You will probably not use more than four input ports

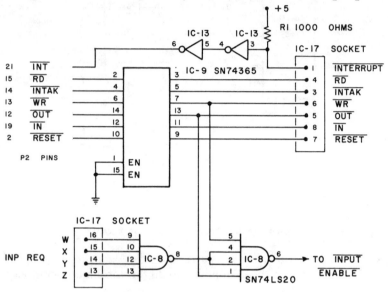

Fig. 5-7. Control circuit schematic.

on the breadboard. Thus, these signals turn the bus around for the input of data only when an input port device select signal is generated on the breadboard, and it is wired by the user to one of the four bus buffer enable inputs.

The "INPUT REQUEST" control pulses are required to be logic zero pulses. They are applied to the pins labeled W, X, Y, and Z, which are pins 16 through 13 on the socket at IC-17.

Table 5-4. Control Signal Connections at IC-17

| Pin (IC-17) | Control Signal | Direction |
|---|---|---|
| 1 | INT | Input |
| 2 | Not Used | ——— |
| 3 | INTAK | Output |
| 4 | RD | Output |
| 5 | OUT | Output |
| 6 | WR | Output |
| 7 | RESET | Output |
| 8 | IN | Output |

The actual ORing of these control signals is performed by the SN74LS20 gate, IC-8. The INPUT REQUEST signal that is output by this 4-input NAND gate is further gated with $\overline{\text{OUT}}$ and $\overline{\text{WR}}$. This gating provides a safety interlock, so that if your breadboard circuits have been improperly wired, the bus drivers cannot be placed in the input mode when an output-type operation is taking place. The resultant "INPUT REQUEST, BUT NOT $\overline{\text{OUT}}$ OR $\overline{\text{WR}}$" signal controls the input/output mode of the 8216 bus buffers.

Since the Apple generates only the memory write signal, $\overline{\text{WR}}$, this simply means that your interface will not be able to turn the bus around for an input operation, when the computer is performing a write operation. The $\overline{\text{OUT}}$ signal is used for interfacing with 8080, 8085, or Z-80 computers.

Two input ports are shown in Fig. 5-8. Each of these ports is controlled by a device select pulse that enables the three-state buffers. This same signal is used as the input request signal, INP REQ, and each input port must generate its own input request signal. In this example, the two input request signals have been connected to the W and Z pins at the INP REQ section of the socket at IC-17. It would have been just as easy to connect the lines to the X and Y pins.

The use of the interlocking INPUT REQUEST signal, and the associated circuitry only applies to testing interface circuits on the breadboard. If you wish to construct an interface that will directly plug into the Apple, and that will not use bidirectional bus buffering, then you will not need to use such an interlock. The main purpose of this circuitry is to protect your Apple computer from possible dam-

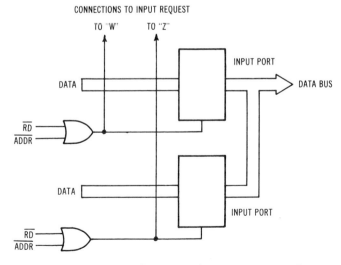

Fig. 5-8. Typical input ports showing use of INPUT REQUEST signal.

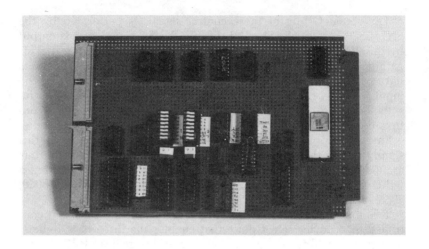

**Fig. 5-9. Wire-wrap version of the interface circuit.**

age caused by careless or incorrect wiring of a test circuit. Once a circuit has been completely tested and debugged, you can probably connect it directly to the data bus of the Apple without any problem.

**Breadboard Construction**

The breadboard circuits may be constructed using wire-wrap techniques, as shown in Fig. 5-9. In this case, the circuits could be expanded and modified through simple wiring changes, but the breadboard itself would be somewhat difficult to use.

To aid in interface construction and testing, a printed circuit has been developed in which all of the necessary circuitry has been placed on a single board. The power supply and logic probe circuitry have been incorporated to make the breadboard easy to use. The breadboard is shown in Fig. 5-10, and is available in kit or assembled form from Group Technology, P.O. Box 87B, Check, VA 24072. A large space has been left unused on the breadboard so that a solderless breadboard socket may be mounted directly on the printed-circuit board for easy experimentation. Typical breadboard sockets are the "SK-10" from E & L Instruments, Derby CT 06418 and the "Super Strip" from AP Products, Inc., Mentor, OH 44060. A complete list of parts needed for the breadboard, along with the printed-circuit board artwork is provided in the Appendix.

## CONNECTIONS TO THE APPLE

Since the interface breadboard uses a 40-conductor cable to connect to various computers, you will need a means of connecting the

Fig. 5-10. Packaged version of the interface. *(Courtesy E&L Instruments, Inc.)*

cable to one of the peripheral interface slots in the Apple. We recommend the use of a flat cable assembly such as shown in Fig. 5-11. There is a printed circuit female edge connector assembly on one end of the cable, and a 0.1-inch by 0.1-inch female pin grid connector on the other. The openings on both connectors must face in the same direction. A ready made cable is available from Group Technology, BG-100-Cable, which uses a two-foot length of flat cable.

The actual connections with the Apple bus signals are made with a small adapter card. This card "twists" and "turns" the various signals so that they are routed from the edge connector to the peripheral connector in the Apple. You can easily put together an adapter by using a Vector 4609 prototype card. This card plugs into one of

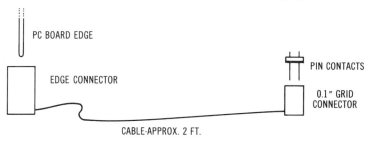

Fig. 5-11. Cable for interface.

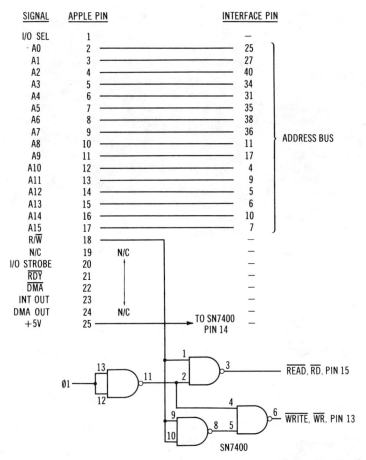

| SIGNAL | APPLE PIN | | | | INTERFACE PIN | |
|---|---|---|---|---|---|---|
| I/O SEL | 1 | | | | — | |
| A0 | 2 | | | | 25 | |
| A1 | 3 | | | | 27 | |
| A2 | 4 | | | | 40 | |
| A3 | 5 | | | | 34 | |
| A4 | 6 | | | | 31 | |
| A5 | 7 | | | | 35 | |
| A6 | 8 | | | | 38 | |
| A7 | 9 | | | | 36 | |
| A8 | 10 | | | | 11 | ADDRESS BUS |
| A9 | 11 | | | | 17 | |
| A10 | 12 | | | | 4 | |
| A11 | 13 | | | | 9 | |
| A12 | 14 | | | | 5 | |
| A13 | 15 | | | | 6 | |
| A14 | 16 | | | | 10 | |
| A15 | 17 | | | | 7 | |
| R/W̄ | 18 | | | | — | |
| N/C | 19 | N/C | | | — | |
| I/O STROBE | 20 | | | | — | |
| R̄D̄Ȳ | 21 | | | | — | |
| D̄M̄Ā | 22 | | | | — | |
| INT OUT | 23 | | | | — | |
| DMA OUT | 24 | N/C | | | — | |
| +5V | 25 | | TO SN7400 PIN 14 | | — | |

READ, RD̄, PIN 15

WRITE, W̄R̄, PIN 13

SN7400

Fig. 5-12. Apple-to-interface

the peripheral connectors in the Apple, and it has a 40-conductor edge connector that will connect directly to the interface cable. Of course, if you wish, you may make direct solder connections to the cable, but we do not recommend this. You can make direct soldered connections between the corresponding signal conductors on each edge connector by using short pieces of hookup wire. If you do not wish to make soldered connections, you can solder wire-wrap pins into the holes provided at each edge connector, making the connections using wire-wrap wire.

The connections are shown in Fig. 5-12. If you choose to use the Vector prototype card, there are several important things that you must do before you start to make the connections between the two edge connectors, no matter which wiring technique you choose to

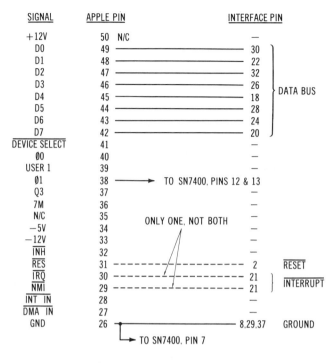

| SIGNAL | APPLE PIN | INTERFACE PIN | |
|---|---|---|---|
| +12V | 50 N/C | — | |
| D0 | 49 —————————— | 30 | |
| D1 | 48 —————————— | 22 | |
| D2 | 47 —————————— | 32 | |
| D3 | 46 —————————— | 26 | |
| D4 | 45 —————————— | 18 | DATA BUS |
| D5 | 44 —————————— | 28 | |
| D6 | 43 —————————— | 24 | |
| D7 | 42 —————————— | 20 | |
| DEVICE SELECT | 41 | — | |
| 00 | 40 | — | |
| USER 1 | 39 | — | |
| 01 | 38 ——————→ TO SN7400, PINS 12 & 13 | | |
| Q3 | 37 | — | |
| 7M | 36 | — | |
| N/C | 35 | — | |
| −5V | 34 | — ONLY ONE, NOT BOTH | |
| −12V | 33 | — | |
| INH | 32 | — | |
| RES | 31 - - - - - - / - - - - - - - - | 2 | RESET |
| IRQ | 30 - - - - - - / - - - - - - - | 21 | INTERRUPT |
| NMI | 29 - - - - - - / - - - - - - - | 21 | |
| INT IN | 28 | — | |
| DMA IN | 27 | — | |
| GND | 26 •—————————————— | 8,29,37 | GROUND |
|  | └→ TO SN7400, PIN 7 | | |

- - - - = OPTIONAL CONNECTION

**connectors connections.**

use. There are probably one or two printed circuit "foil runs," or conductor paths between the 40-conductor connector and the +5-volt and ground contact pins on the 50-conductor Apple connector. All such connections must be broken, so that the 40-conductor connector contacts are "free," and uncommitted to any signals. You can use a small razor knife to cut these connectors. We recommend making two cuts through each conductor, about 2 or 3 millimeters apart. A soldering iron can then be used to "lift" the cutout section by heating it. You should do this to only the power connections which are connected between the two connectors. All of the other pins are "free."

Since the Vector prototype board does not use plated-through holes, be sure that you connect +5 volts and ground to the respective power buses, and that the proper connections are made to the SN7400 chip.

The SN7400 chip is used to gate the read/write ($R/\overline{W}$) signal with the main clock signal of the 6502 processor, $\Phi 1$. This gating generates the memory read signal, $\overline{RD}$, and the memory write signal, $\overline{WR}$. If this gating is not done, the computer peripherals on the interface breadboard will not work properly. In some computers, there are separate read and write signals. If you wish to use separate read and write signals for memory control in the Apple and other computer systems that are based on the 6502 microprocessor chip, you must generate them through the proper gating.

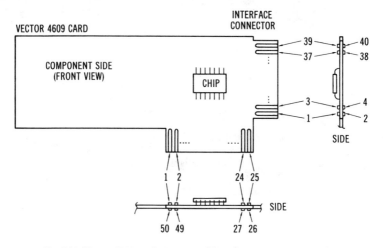

Fig. 5-13. Vector 4609 card contacts and interface contact arrangements.

The pin locations for the Vector card edge connectors are shown in Fig. 5-13. Please note that this figure shows the *component side* of the card. Once you have made the needed connections between the two edge connectors, and between the connectors and the SN7400, we suggest that you use an ohmmeter or other continuity-checking instrument, to be sure that there are no short circuits between adjacent and opposite pins, and that the correct connections have been made. These tests should be made with the SN7400 chip *out of its socket*. However, don't forget to plug it back in after you have tested the connections!

## OTHER CONSIDERATIONS

If you wish to try and interface some of the 6502 family interface chips, and even some of the nonfamily chips, you will find that these chips have rather slow access times when compared to the standard three-state input chips, such as the SN74365 and the SN74LS244. Access times for these large, programmable chips can be as long as 200 ns. Since the read/write timing for the 6502 chip is fairly critical, there will not be sufficient time for the data from these chips to be accessed and placed on the bus if the extra delay caused by the 8216 bus buffer chips and the interlocking circuits is taken into account. Therefore, if you wish to use the breadboard to test interface circuits that use complex, programmable interface chips, you will need to "defeat" the interlock. You can do this rather simply by removing the two 8216 bus buffer chips and by using short jumper wires at each socket to connect the Apple data bus signals to the interface data bus lines. For example, you would need a jumper between pins 5 and 6, pins 2 and 3, pins 14 and 13, and pins 9 and 10 on each socket. We refer you to Fig. 5-5 for the circuit that uses the 8216 bus buffer chips.

A word of caution is in order, however. By removing the bus buffer chips, you are connecting your interface circuits directly onto the Apple data bus. Please use extreme caution when doing this so that you do not cause any short circuits or bus conflicts in the Apple. We have provided a simple interface example in Chapter 7 in which the direct bus interfacing is used.

CHAPTER **6**

# Apple Interface
# Experiments

The purpose of the experiments in this section is to provide you
with some hands-on experience in the use of latched output port and
three-state input port circuits that were developed in the previous
chapters. You will find that these experiments use simple SN7400-
series devices to transfer data to and from the Apple.

### INTRODUCTION TO THE EXPERIMENTS

Breadboarding of circuits will be required in this chapter, and a
complete list of parts that will be used is provided in Appendix B.
We have assumed that you have had some experience in breadboarding simple logic circuits, and that you are familiar with the basic
breadboarding skills. Some auxiliary functions will be required in
the experiments to both monitor logic states and to generate them.
In general, we use lamp monitors or LEDs to indicate logic one (on)
and logic zero (off), logic switches to generate logic levels, and debounced pulsers, or pulsers for short, to generate logic levels with
clean noise-free transitions between the logic levels. Some simple
schematic diagrams of these types of circuits are provided in the
Appendix. If you do not wish to build these circuits, they can be
breadboarded separately, or similar functions can be purchased from
companies such as E & L Instruments, Derby, CT 06418 or PAC-
COM, Redmond, WA 98052. In general, most of the experiments in
this book can be done with a few simple circuits.

We have provided one experiment that illustrates the use of a
decoder circuit for device addressing. While many decoder schemes

are possible, we think that one experiment should illustrate the basic principles. If you are interested in other decoder circuits, there are many different ones described in *8085A Cookbook,* and *Programming & Interfacing the 6502, With Experiments* (Howard W. Sams & Co., Inc., Indianapolis, IN 46268). Actually, memory and I/O device addressing is pretty much the same, from one computer to the next. In most interface circuits, the decoder circuit that is used on the interface breadboard will work quite well.

While this book tackles Apple interfacing at a fairly low level, there are other important interfacing topics that you might wish to study. Many of these are covered in *TRS-80® Interfacing, Book 2* (Howard W. Sams & Co., Inc., Indianapolis, IN 46268). The information presented is fairly general, and it is easily applied to Apple computer systems. Topics covered include: high-current, high-voltage load driving, digital-to-analog and analog-to-digital converters, practical data processing (smoothing, filtering, averaging, etc.), serial communications, and remote control.

The photograph in Fig. 6-1 shows a typical Apple-breadboard laboratory station that is used in performing the experiments in this chapter. A 40-conductor cable has been used to connect the breadboard and the Apple computer—Fig. 6-2. This cable has been described in Chapter 5. When you connect the interface breadboard to the Apple, be sure that the cable is oriented properly. *The cable must point away from the component side of the card used to connect the interface to the Apple.* At the interface-breadboard end of

**Fig. 6-1. Apple computer and breadboard in experimental use.**

Fig. 6-2. Interface cable. (Note connector orientation on same side of flat cable.)

the cable, the cable must be pushed onto the 40 pins so that the cable is pointed either down or away from the printed-circuit board. If the cable is connected improperly, the Apple will respond with a screen full of random characters rather than the APPLE II banner, when it is first turned on. This does not seem to cause any permanent damage to the Apple or to the interface as long as they are not connected this way for too long.

Some experiments will build on, or use, the circuits or programs developed in previous experiments. Please do not turn off the power to the computer, and do not disconnect circuits until you are told to do so, otherwise, you will spend a great deal of time reloading programs and reconstructing interface circuits. There will be a reminder at the end of some of the experiments just so that you don't forget this tip.

Most readers will probably perform the experiments in sequence, so there will not be too much difficulty in referring back to previous experiments for the details of the interface circuits. However, if you choose to skip over some experiments you may find this a bit confusing. To help everyone with the interface circuits, we have reproduced the important input port, output port, and control circuits in Fig. 6-27 *at the end of this chapter.* You can make a photocopy of this figure, or you may remove it from the book so that it will be nearby when you need it. The basic circuits shown in this figure are used in most of the experiments unless otherwise noted, and you can use these circuits to build general-purpose input and output ports as you need them.

If you are an instructor planning to use this book as the basis for laboratory experiments with the Apple, you will find that the programs are easily loaded onto cassettes. In this way the programs are readily available for the students, who do not have to spend their time trying to debug programs. If you choose to use cassettes, you should use high quality tape, and once the programs have been recorded on the tape, the "write protect" tab on the back edge of the cassette should be removed. This will prevent students from accidentally recording programs over those already on tape.

Students may find it valuable to maintain cassettes of their own, so that their lab solutions and other programs are readily available, either for exchange with other students or lab groups, or for reference during the next lab period.

The experiments in this chapter have been divided into two groups, although no division, chapter subheading, or other note marks the sections. The first 11 experiments provide a basic set of interfacing and programming investigations for readers who are interested in basic interfacing concepts. These first experiments provide a basis for the laboratory portion of a first course in computer interfacing and computer electronics.

The last few experiments provide additional lab investigations into more advanced topics, and they also provide projects that may be used to supplement the basic set of experiments. Of course, all of the experiments may be done, too.

## EXPERIMENT NO. 1
## USE OF THE LOGIC PROBE

### Purpose

The purpose of this experiment is to show you how the logic probe circuit on the breadboard may be used to detect logic levels and pulses.

### Discussion

We have assumed that you are using the breadboard logic probe, although other logic-probe circuits will work equally well. The steps in this experiment are useful in helping you to become familiar with the breadboard and the signals available.

### Step 1

Your Apple computer should be connected to its video monitor and also to the interface breadboard through the 40-conductor cable.

This connection has been described in the introduction to the experiments.

Turn on the power to the Apple and to the breadboard. The computer should print "APPLE II" and the flashing square cursor should be seen. If this is not the case, turn off the power and check your connections. Be sure that the 40-conductor cable is securely pushed onto the pins at the interface breadboard and onto the edge of the board that connects it to the Apple. You should also check the orientation of the cable to be sure that it is correct. If you cannot locate the problem, obtain assistance.

### Step 2

With the power applied to the breadboard, connect a jumper wire between one of the logic probe input pins, P, at the PROBE socket, and one of the +5-volt power pins at the power socket. What is the effect on the logic probe indicators?

The red LED is on, indicating the presence of the logic one state.

The probe jumper wire should now be moved from the +5-volt power pin to one of the ground pins on the same power socket. What is observed, once this connection is made?

The green LED is on, indicating the presence of a logic zero state at the input to the probe circuit. You may have noticed that the pulse detecting LED (yellow) flashed as you made the connection to +5 volts or to ground. This flash indicates that the probe detected a *change* in the logic level. Either a logic-one-to-logic-zero, or a logic-zero-to-logic-one transition will cause the yellow LED to flash. This makes it particularly useful for detecting pulses and logic transitions.

Connect the probe input to address line A0 at IC-19. What do you observe when this connection has been made? All of the LEDs are on, probably at different intensities. This is due to the fact that the 6502 microprocessor chip is executing many, many assembly-language instructions in the BASIC and monitor ROMs, thus using the address bus to address various memory locations. Move the logic probe test wire to the other address bus lines, A1, A2, and A3. You should be able to detect similar "activity" at these pins, too.

## Step 3

You may wish to test other points on the breadboard with the logic probe. The data bus lines and the control signals may be easily tested. You should keep in mind that the logic probe is only sensitive to the logic levels presented by the outputs of standard transistor-transistor logic (TTL) chips used on the breadboard and in the experiments. *Do not* attempt to use the probe to measure anything but these logic levels. If you connect the probe to voltages outside the zero to +5-volt range, the probe circuit will be damaged.

## Step 4

When you use the probe, you will notice that there are many combinations of lit LEDs. For example, you may see that the red and yellow LEDs are lit, while the green one is unlit. Do you have an idea of what this means?

This means that a pulse is being detected, *and* that the *normal* logic level of the circuit being tested is a logic one. The green LED lights very briefly (you can't see it), to indicate the fleeting presence of the logic zero pulse. The pulse detecting circuit stretches the pulse and lights the yellow LED so that you can "see" that a pulse has been "caught."

You may also see the green and yellow LEDs on, with the red LED off. What would this indicate?

A logic zero level would be indicated, with short logic one pulses.

It is possible that all LEDs may be lit, too. In this case, the input to the logic probe is rapidly changing between logic one and logic zero.

In some of the following experiments, the logic probe will be used to examine outputs and to detect logic states and pulses. This will be noted by, ". . . use your probe to examine. . . ," or perhaps by, ". . . use the logic probe to measure . . . ." This simply means that you are to connect the logic probe to the circuit being tested, so that you can "see" what is happening.

Turn your computer off.

# EXPERIMENT NO 2
## USE OF THE DEVICE ADDRESS DECODER

### Purpose

This experiment allows you to explore the use of the device address decoder circuit on the interface breadboard printed-circuit
board. Since this decoder will be used in all of the experiments, you
must have a good understanding of its use.

### Discussion

In this experiment, address bits A15-A0 will be used to identify
specific addresses for use by I/O devices. The address switches will
be set up for a specific range of addresses, and the logic probe will
be used to examine the action of the decoder circuit. You will also
use an SN7402 NOR gate integrated circuit.

### Pin Configuration of the Integrated Circuit (Fig. 6-3)

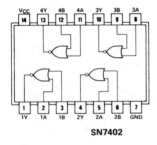

SN7402

Fig. 6-3. SN7402 NOR-gate pin configuration.

### Step 1

No circuits should be presently wired on your breadboard. If there
are any circuits present, remove them from the solderless breadboard. In this experiment, the entire 16-bit address bus will be used
by the decoder section of the interface. Be sure that the bottom
switch at the LO address dip switch (IC-6) is in the "M" position,
or in the "ON" position.

### Step 2

Place the dip switches for all of the address bits, A15-A4, in the
logic one position. Remember not to change the setting of the "M"
switch. Can you determine which set of addresses will be decoded
by the SN74154 decoder? What addresses in this block will be available at the ADDRESS output socket? You may wish to examine the
schematic in Fig. 5-4.

Addresses in the block from 65520 to 65535 will be decoded by the 4-to-16 decoder (SN74154). Since the decoder only provides you with the "bottom" eight addresses, only addresses from 65520 to 65527 will be available.

## Step 3

Turn your computer on. If you are running a program, press the RESET key. Use the logic probe to test the eight address outputs at the ADDRESS socket. Are any of the decoder outputs active (pulsing)? Since you are not running a program, is this what you would expect?

Two of the outputs should be active, 0 and 4, corresponding to addresses 65520 and 65524. While the computer is not running a BASIC program, it is executing many assembly-language steps that monitor the keyboard, etc. Remember that the address decoding circuitry is *always* decoding addresses.

## Step 4

Wire the circuit shown in Fig. 6-4. Be sure that you connect the power pin, pin 14, to +5 volts and the ground pin, pin 7, to power

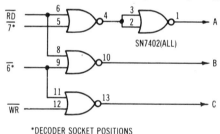

*DECODER SOCKET POSITIONS

**Fig. 6-4. Function pulse-generation circuit.**

ground. Refer to Fig. 6-3 for the pin configuration of the SN7402. You may substitute an SN74LS02 for this chip. The outputs of the gates, A, B, and C, are not connected to any circuit at this time.

## Step 5

Change the switch settings on the dip switches for bits A15-A4 for an address of 49312. This is $11000000\ 10100000_2$, and you should ignore the four least-significant bits. What range of addresses will be available when the address switches are set this way?

Addresses from 49312 through 49327 will be decoded, but only addresses 49312 through 49319 will be available.

**Step 6**

Enter the following program into the computer and run it:

```
10  A = PEEK(49318)
20  GOTO 10
```

Using the logic probe, monitor the outputs of the decoder, and note your observations below:

You should see that the "6" output is active, and one or more other outputs may be active, too.

Now monitor the outputs of the gates, A, B, and C, and note any activity, at these points, as determined with the logic probe, in the space below:

| | Logic 0 | Logic 1 | Pulse |
|---|---|---|---|
| A | | | |
| B | | | |
| C | | | |

Is this what you would expect? Can you explain this?

Yes, this is what is expected, since the input (PEEK) command is the program specified device 49318 as an input device, and the decoded address is found at the "6" output from the decoder. Thus, only output "B" should be active. No other input devices were specified in the program, and no output devices were specified, either.

**Step 7**

Change the device address in line 10 so that address 49325 is selected. Line 10 should now be 10 A=PEEK(49325). Run the program and test the gate outputs A, B, and C once again. Are any of the outputs active, indicating the presence of pulses? Why?

None of the outputs should be active, since device address 49325 has not been implemented in the circuit. Furthermore, address 49325 is not readily available on the breadboard. Of the addresses in the block 49312 through 49327, only addresses 49312 through 49319 are available at the ADDRESS socket.

## Step 8

Change line 10 in the program so that it is now

```
10   A = PEEK(49318):B = PEEK(49319)
```

Where do you observe the pulses in the circuit when you run the modified program?

You should find that outputs A and B are active. Output C is not active since it is an output control pulse, and there are no output (POKE) commands in the program.

## Step 9

Make another modification to your program. Change line 10 so that you can control output device 49318. Your statement at line 10 should look like this:

```
10   POKE 49318,0
```

You can use any data value that is between 0 and 255, inclusive. Now run your program and test outputs A, B, and C. Which output do you expect to be active? Is this what you found?

Output C is active, since the POKE command is an output-type command, and the address, 49318, corresponds to the "6" output pin from the decoder. You are probably surprised to see that the B output is also active. When a POKE instruction is executed by the BASIC interpreter in the Apple, the computer system does a read-before-write operation, so that the selected address is read from, before being written to. This must be kept in mind during the design of interface circuits.

**Step 10**

Could you reconfigure the switches in the address decoder section so that addresses 50944 through 50951 are generated by the decoder? How would you attempt to do this? Are these addresses really going to be available?

Yes, you could change the switch settings to allow the decoder to operate between these addresses. First, convert the first address into its binary equivalent: 50944 = 11000111 00000000. Second, make the changes in the switch settings for A15-A8 and for A7-A4. Now, what addresses would correspond to the "6" and "7" outputs from the decoder? Test your answers by using PEEK commands in the simple program that you have been using in this experiment. You should be able to see the pulses at the A and B outputs from the gates.

*Once you have tested this, be sure to return the address switches to their previous settings, corresponding to the binary value, 11000000 10100000.*

Do not remove the circuit from your breadboard. It will be used again. The program will not be used, however, so you may turn off the power to your breadboard and computer.

## EXPERIMENT NO. 3
## USING DEVICE-SELECT PULSES

**Purpose**

In this experiment, you will observe the use of device-select pulses to control an external device. Although generally used to control the flow of information, the PEEK and POKE commands may also be used to generate useful pulses to simply control external devices.

**Discussion**

In this experiment, a simple device will be turned on and off through the use of device select pulses. The logic probe will be used as the "device," and a simple flip-flop will be controlled by two software-generated pulses.

## Pin Configuration of the Integrated Circuits (Fig. 6-5)

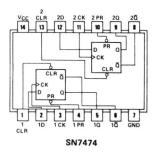

Fig. 6-5. SN7402 and SN7474 chip pin configurations.

### Step 1

The device select circuit used in Experiment No. 2 is also used in this experiment. If it has not been wired, wire it as shown in Fig. 6-4.

### Step 2

Wire the SN7474 flip-flop as shown in Fig. 6-6. The "1" noted at the "D" input to the SN7474 means that a logic one (+5 volts) is applied to this input. Likewise, a "0" would indicate a logic zero, or ground connection. The 0 and 1 notations are used to distinguish logic level connections from power-carrying connections. The Q output from the flip-flop should be the only device connected to the logic probe. Remember to make the power connections to the SN7474 flip-flop; pin 14 to +5 volts and pin 7 to ground.

### Step 3

In this circuit, the WR 49318 pulse (signal C) will clock the output of the flip-flop to a logic one, while the $\overline{RD\ 49319}$ pulse (signal A) will clear it to a logic zero. Since a flip-flop is stable in either state, once pulsed by RD 49319, its Q output will remain in the logic one

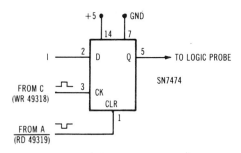

Fig. 6-6. Simple flip-flop controller circuit.

state until power is removed, or until it is cleared to logic zero with a $\overline{\text{WR}}$ 49318 pulse.

```
Enter the following program in to your computer and run it.
10   A = PEEK(49319)
20   POKE 49318,0
30   FOR T = TO 300: NEXT T
40   A = PEEK(49319)
50   FOR T = 0 TO 300: NEXT T
60   GOTO 20
```

Disregard the flashing of the logic probe pulse LED. What is the effect on the logic one and logic zero LEDs?

They flash logic one, logic zero, logic one, etc., in sequence.

## Step 4

Alter the time delay routine at line 50 to:

```
50   FOR T = 0 TO 1000: NEXT T
```

When this change has been made, run the program. What is the effect of this simple program change?

The logic zero LED is on for a longer period. Thus, it is possible to generate control pulses that are a known period apart, say 1 second.

## Step 5

Can you determine the software delay necessary in a FOR . . . : NEXT T statement to generate a 1-second period? Modify your program and test various delay counts until you closely approximate 1 second. You might want to try for a 10-second period and then divide the count by 10 for a 1-second period. What delay count did you come up with? We found that a delay statement,

```
FOR T = 0 TO 780: NEXT T
```

required about 1 second to be executed.

## Step 6

You can now use the power of BASIC to allow you to tell the computer how long each LED is to be ON. The following program may be entered and run. It first asks you for the period of each LED, in seconds, and then runs the program.

```
10   A = PEEK(49319)
20   INPUT "RED LED PERIOD ";Q
30   INPUT  "  GREEN LED PERIOD "; R
40   PRINT "TOTAL CYCLE PERIOD "; Q+R; " SECONDS"
50   POKE 49318,0
60   FOR S = 1 TO Q
70   FOR T = 0 TO 780: NEXT T
80   NEXT S
90   A = PEEK(49319)
100  FOR S = 1 TO R
110  FOR T = 0 TO 780: NEXT T
120  NEXT S
130  GOTO 50
```

When the program is run, the time delays may be somewhat lengthened. Why?

The additional software steps (FOR S = 1 TO Q, FOR S = 1 TO R and NEXT S), add time to the overall execution time of the program, although you will not see appreciable lengthening of the program.

What does this program show you?

It illustrates many principles; the use of simple programs and simple circuits to control external devices. It also illustrates the power of BASIC to control external devices through relatively simple software steps. Remember, though, that BASIC is relatively slow.

Even though PEEK and POKE commands were used, the success of the flip-flop interface *did not depend on the actual transfer of any data or information.* The flip-flop was controlled, or switched, through the use of device select pulses, alone. This principle is often used when a control signal or control pulse is required, but no data is transferred.

Please remember that when a POKE command is used in the BASIC interpreter in the APPLE computer, *a read and a write operation are* performed. Thus, if you choose to use a POKE command to generate a device select pulse for control purposes, *you must remember that the APPLE will also perform a read from the same address.*

If you are using two control pulses with the same address, say, WR XYZ and RD XYZ, the RD XYZ will also be activated during a write operation caused by a POKE XYZ command.

The SN7474 flip-flop circuit may be removed from your breadboard, but the SN7402 circuit should be retained. The program will not be used again, so you may remove power from your system.

**EXPERIMENT NO. 4**
**CONSTRUCTING AN INPUT PORT**

### Purpose

The purpose of this experiment is to construct an input port using three-state buffer circuits.

### Discussion

The simple 8-bit input port that you will construct as a part of this experiment will provide a means of entering data into the computer. Several additional experiments will use this input port. The device select circuit used previously will be used in this experiment. The SN74365 or DM8095 three-state buffer chips will be used in this experiment.

### Pin Configuration of the Integrated Circuit (Fig. 6-7)

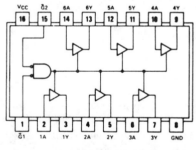

Fig. 6-7. SN74365, or DM8095 three-state buffer chip pin configuration.

SN74365A
SN74LS365

### Step 1

The gating circuit developed in Experiment No. 2 will be used in this experiment. If this circuit is not present on your breadboard, refer to Fig. 6-4 for the circuit details, and wire the circuit shown. Your computer and breadboard power should be off.

### Step 2

Wire the 8-bit input port circuit shown in Fig. 6-8. Two SN74365 (DM8095) three-state integrated circuits are required.

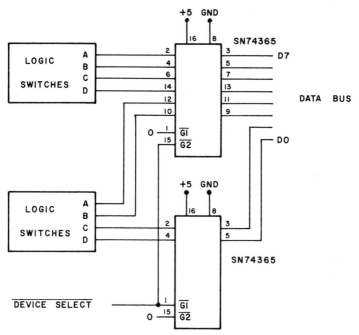

Fig. 6-8. Simple 8-bit input port.

## Step 3

Note that in this circuit only one of the two enabling inputs to the three-state buffer chips has been used. The unused input has been grounded, or connected to logic zero. Thus, the internal gate will not be used for combining a function pulse and a device address. The enabling signal will simply be transferred through the gate to the three-state buffer circuits within the chip.

Connect the $\overline{\text{DEVICE SELECT}}$ line to point A (pin 1 on the SN7402), as shown in Fig. 6-4. This is the signal for $\overline{\text{RD 49319}}$.

The notation LOGIC SWITCHES in Fig. 6-8 is used to represent switches that can generate logic one or logic zero signals at the eight individual inputs to the input port. Simple jumper wires to the +5-volt and ground power supply buses may be used. There is additional information in the Appendix about this type of logic function.

## Step 4

Once the input port has been constructed and the device select pulse has been provided from the SN7402 NOR gate, enter and run the following test program:

```
10  PRINT PEEK(49319): GOTO 10
```

What is displayed on the screen when the program is running? Does changing the logic switches have any effect on the displayed value? Is this what you would expect?

The value 255 is displayed, corresponding to $11111111_2$. Changing the logic switches had no effect on the values that were displayed. At first, you might have expected the values to change as you changed the switch settings, but this was not observed. Why?

The interface circuit was not provided with an input request ($\overline{\text{INP REQ}}$) signal that is used to place the two bus buffers in the input mode.

**Step 5**

Make a connection between the SN7402 A, or $\overline{\text{RD 49319}}$, signal and the W input at the INP REQ section of the CONTROL SIGNALS socket. This signal will place the 8216 bus buffers in the input mode.

Now that this connection has been made, restart your program and change the switch settings. Are the changes in the switch settings shown as changes in the numbers being displayed? You should test several different settings.

The switch values are now transferred to the computer, converted into decimal numbers and displayed on the monitor screen.

If you would rather see the values in binary form, the following program may be run. It will display the binary numbers continuously.

```
10   A = 128
20   B = PEEK(49319)
30   FOR Q = 1 TO 8
40   IF B−A<0 THEN GOTO 100
50   PRINT "1";
60   B = B−A
65   A = A/2
70   NEXT Q
75   PRINT
80   GOTO 10
```

```
100   PRINT "0";
110   GOTO 65
```

If you wish to change a switch setting and *then* obtain its binary equivalent, change line 10 to:

```
10   INPUT A$: HOME: A = 128
```

Now, whenever you wish to display the binary value of the logic switch setting at the input port, simply depress the RETURN key on the Apple keyboard. Of course, the switch settings are already in binary format, so the correlation between the displayed binary value and the individual bits at the input port should be easy.

Do not remove the circuit from your breadboard, and do not turn off the power. Both the program and the circuit will be used in the next experiment.

**EXPERIMENT NO. 5**
**MULTIBYTE INPUT PORTS**

**Purpose**

The purpose of this experiment is to show you how multiple bytes of information may be input and processed by a BASIC program.

**Discussion**

Not all input devices transfer only one byte of information to the Apple computer. Some devices may require 9 or more bits. In this experiment, you will simulate two input ports through the use of the input port that was constructed in Experiment No. 4. Refer to Experiment No. 4 for construction details of the input port. We recommend that you work through Experiment No. 4 before proceeding with this experiment, if you have not already performed it.

**Step 1**

If you do not have an input port connected to your Apple computer, we refer you to Experiment No. 4. The circuit developed in that experiment must be used.

**Step 2**

In handling multibyte data, the Apple must be programmed so that the various bytes are ordered from most-significant to least-significant byte. In this experiment, we shall use byte "M" as the most-significant byte (MSBY) and "L" as the least-significant byte (LSBY). Since the Apple will interpret 8-bit values as decimal numbers between 0 and 255, can you suggest an equation or series of operations that can be used to obtain the decimal equivalent for a two-byte binary number?

Since the MSBY is "offset" by a factor of 256, you can use the following relationship:

VALUE = (M * 256) + L

where VALUE is the final decimal value of the 16-bit word.

## Step 3

To test this equation, enter the following program into the computer:

```
200   INPUT "SET MSBY ON SWITCHES ";A$
210   M = PEEK(49319)
220   INPUT "SET LSBY ON SWITCHES ";A$
230   L = PEEK (49319)
240   V = (256 * M) + L
250   PRINT V
260   GOTO 200
```

Now run the program, starting it by entering GOTO 200, and pressing the RETURN key. When the computer asks, "SET MSBY ON SWITCHES?" set the eight bits for the value of the MSBY on the eight switches. Depress the RETURN key on the keyboard. When the computer asks, "SET LSBY ON SWITCHES?" change the eight switches so that they represent the eight bits that you wish to enter for the LSBY value. When the switches have been set, depress the RETURN key so that the computer will know that you are ready. Now the decimal value should be displayed on the video monitor. Some typical 16-bit values that you might wish to try are listed below. Fill in the decimal value for each, as generated by the Apple. You should be able to check these fairly quickly with the aid of a calculator.

| MSBY | LSBY | VALUE |
|------|------|-------|
| 11001010 | 11000001 | |
| 11000111 | 00011101 | |
| 00000001 | 10000001 | |

You should find values of 51905, 50973, and 385.

## Step 4

The following program is a combination of the binary output program, and the two-byte decimal calculation program. It will allow you to input two 8-bit bytes to represent a 16-bit value, display the decimal value and the binary value.

```
10   A = 32768
20   FOR S = 1 TO 2
30   FOR Q = 1 TO 8
40   IF B−A<0 THEN GOTO 100
50   PRINT "1";
60   B = B−A
65   A = A/2
70   NEXT Q
75   PRINT "     ";:NEXT S
80   PRINT: GOTO 200
100  PRINT "0";
110  GOTO 65
200  INPUT "SET MSBY ON SWITCHES "; A$
210  M = PEEK(49319)
220  INPUT "SET LSBY ON SWITCHES "; A$
230  L = PEEK(49319)
240  V = (256 * M) + L
250  HOME: PRINT V
260  B = V: GOTO 10
```

## Step 5

Run the program by entering a GOTO 200 command and then depressing the RETURN key. Set values for the MSBY and LSBY on the switches. There should be a correlation between your switch settings and the binary bits that are displayed on the screen. You should be able to convert the binary value into a decimal value fairly easily. The 16-bit binary value has been "split" into two 8-bit values so that you can easily compare the bits with your switch settings.

Now that you have seen how the Apple can operate on two 8-bit bytes to reconstruct a 16-bit value, you should realize that other types of operations could have been performed, too. Although only a single-input port has been used in this experiment, it would be easy to construct another one with a new device address to provide the additional byte of data required in the 16-bit application that has been simulated in this experiment.

You probably noticed that a new variable, A$, was used in this experiment, and in the last one. This is a "dummy" variable that has been used so that the program can be halted at a predetermined point so that the experimental conditions could be changed before the computer is allowed to go on. The A$ variable is a string variable, and when the RETURN key is pressed a null, or "nothing," string of characters is assigned to this variable. This is just a "trick" that halts the computer until we depress the RETURN key.

The interface circuit used in this experiment will be used in the following experiment, so it should be saved. The software will not be used, so the computer and interface may be turned off.

## EXPERIMENT NO. 6
## INPUT PORT APPLICATIONS

### Purpose

The purpose of this experiment is to show you how an input port may be used for control applications.

### Discussion

In this experiment, the 8-bit input port will be used to transfer information to the Apple, but the Apple will process the eight bits of data in a nonnumeric fashion. In this way, the *state* of eight external devices will be monitored.

### Step 1

If you do not have an input port connected to your Apple computer, we refer you to Experiment No. 4. The input port described in that experiment will be used in the following steps.

### Step 2

In many cases, the computer will be used to process nonnumeric information that tells the computer about the status or state of external devices. In such a way, it is easy to determine when devices are on or off, valves open or closed, elevators up or down, and so on.

Enter the following program into your computer and run it. This program demonstrates how a value may be used to cause the computer to take a preprogrammed course of action:

```
10   INPUT A$: HOME
20   A = PEEK(49319)
30   IF A>127 THEN GOTO 70
40   PRINT "INPUT <= 127"
50   GOTO 10
70   PRINT "INPUT > 127"
80   GOTO 10
```

### Step 3

You must press the RETURN key to cause the computer to execute the input and comparison steps. Set the logic switches at the input port to a value that is less than 127 ( 00000000 to 01111110 ) and press RETURN. What happens? Try this with a value of 127 or greater ( 01111111 to 11111111 ). What happens? What happens when the binary value is equal to 127 ( 01111111 )? You should see the correct message for each value that is input to the computer. This program illustrates how the computer can be used to make a decision based upon a value. In some cases, the value of an individual bit may be used as the basis for a decision. The binary conversion program provided in Experiment No. 4 allowed you to see a binary equivalent for a decimal value. This program made decisions based upon the value of individual bits, so that it could determine whether to display a one in each bit position.

## Step 4

In this step, the basic binary-display routine will be used, but rather than display ones and zeros, the computer will display "ON," for a logic one and "OFF," for a logic zero. You should be able to modify the program from Experiment No. 4 to do this, just by changing the PRINT statements, but the following program is provided for you. Note that the program from Experiment No. 4 has been "moved," or relocated to higher line numbers. Before you enter this program, remember to delete the old one, if you have not already done so by turning off the power. The NEW command may be used to delete the old program. Simply type NEW and then press the RETURN key.

```
410   INPUT A$: HOME: A = 128
420   B = PEEK (49319)
430   FOR Q = 1 TO 8
440   IF B-A <0 THEN GOTO 500
450   PRINT "ON  ";
460   B = B-A
470   A = A/2
480   NEXT Q
490   GOTO 410
500   PRINT "OFF ";
510   GOTO 470
```

Note: There are two spaces after ON, and one space after OFF. This generates equal spacing.

Run the program. Remember that the switches should be set, and then the RETURN key pressed, to perform the "conversion" and display. You should see that a line of ON and OFF messages is displayed, with the ON notation for the logic one bits, and the OFF notation for the logic zero bits. The PRINT statements in the program could be changed to display OPEN and CLOSED, UP and DOWN, and other similar notations for the bits.

## Step 5

While the simple program in Step 4 has some uses, the display of the ON and OFF messages in column format may be more useful.

The HTAB and VTAB commands in BASIC may be used to generate such a vertical display of the conditions. The same basic program is used, with the necessary changes marked (*). You need to leave the spaces after ON and OFF in lines 450 and 500, respectively.

```
*400   H = 20: V = 8
 410   INPUT A$: HOME : A = 128
 420   B = PEEK(49319)
 430   FOR Q = 1 TO 8
 440   IF B−A<0 THEN GOTO 500
*450   HTAB H: VTAB V: PRINT "ON ";
 460   B = B−A
*470   A = A/2: V = V+1
 480   NEXT Q
*490   GOTO 400
*500   HTAB H: VTAB V: PRINT "OFF ";
 510   GOTO 470
```

You should now observe that the display of ON and OFF conditions is vertical, since the HTAB and VTAB commands have been used to "move" the cursor in a vertical fashion.

Thus, the ON and OFF conditions can be displayed in a number of ways. In fact, in some computers, graphical representations and alphanumeric characters may be mixed so that the ON/OFF conditions may be displayed near a pictorial representation of the device or process being monitored.

While the program is running, make changes to the switch settings to confirm that the program and the input port are working properly.

**Step 6**

You may want to run the program continuously, so that the switches may be changed, and the ON/OFF conditions monitored, without the need to press the RETURN key each time a new display is needed. The INPUT A$ is the "dummy" input command that causes the computer to stop and wait for you to press the RETURN key. Remove this statement from the program, so that line 410 looks like this:

```
410   HOME: A = 128
```

Now run the program. Does this provide a reasonable display? Why?

Our display flickered badly, since the HOME command clears the entire screen and positions the cursor in the upper left-hand corner of the monitor screen each time the computer restarts the program. This takes time, and it slows down the display. Can you suggest any further changes to the program to reduce or eliminate the flicker?

## Step 7

By removing the HOME command, you can reduce the time that the Apple takes to clear the entire screen and "home" the cursor to the upper left-hand corner of the video display area. When the HTAB and VTAB commands are used, they position the cursor at exactly the right place to print each ON or OFF on each line, one per bit. If no spaces are left after the "ON" at line 450, the printing of the ON would not cover the last F in OFF, and you would see ONF, instead of ON. Thus, the spaces are needed to "erase" any characters remaining on a line.

We suggest that you use the following for line 410 in your program:

```
410  A = 128
```

Now, start the program by typing in HOME:GOTO 400, and then pressing ENTER. If you do not use the HOME command, the program will simply write over whatever is on the screen. The HOME command clears the screen for you just before the program is started.

## Step 8

The VTAB and HTAB commands can also be used to generate titles or captions for each of the eight lines of information in the display. Several captions follow, and you may add or change the ones provided:

```
 5   HOME
10   VTAB 8: HTAB 1
15   PRINT "ACID PUMP";
20   VTAB 9: HTAB 1
25   PRINT "BASE PUMP";
30   VTAB 10: HTAB 1
35   PRINT "HEATER";
40   VTAB 11: HTAB 1
45   PRINT "MIXER";
50   VTAB 12: HTAB 1
55   PRINT  "FLUSH CYCLE";
60   VTAB 13: HTAB 1
65   PRINT "DISHWASHER";
70   VTAB 14: HTAB 1
```

```
75  PRINT "VACUUM":
80  VTAB 15: HTAB 1
85  PRINT "DRYER";
```

We suggest that you add these lines to your program if you plan to go ahead with Experiment No. 7. You should test your program after you add these lines.

The hardware and the software used in this experiment will be used in the next experiment, so you should not dismantle your circuit, nor should you remove power to the computer.

## EXPERIMENT NO. 7
## INPUT PORT APPLICATIONS (II)

### Purpose

The purpose of this experiment is to show you how logical operations may be performed on data.

### Discussion

This experiment will use AND operations, and they will be performed on the ON/OFF information from eight external "sensors." The conditions of these sensors will be used to trigger actions in the computer.

### Step 1

The program used in this experiment is the same as the one used in Experiment No. 6. If it has not been completely entered into your computer, you must enter it and test it. If it has been entered and tested in the previous experiment, you may wish to check it against the following listing:

```
  5  HOME
 10  VTAB 8: HTAB 1
 15  PRINT "ACID PUMP";
 20  VTAB 9: HTAB 1
 25  PRINT "BASE PUMP";
 30  VTAB 10:  HTAB 1
 35  PRINT "HEATER";
 40  VTAB 11:  HTAB 1
 45  PRINT "MIXER";
 50  VTAB 12:  HTAB 1
 55  PRINT "FLUSH CYCLE";
 60  VTAB 13: HTAB 1
 65  PRINT "DISHWASHER";
 70  VTAB 14: HTAB 1
 75  PRINT "VACUUM";
 80  VTAB 15:  HTAB 1
 85  PRINT "DRYER";
400  H = 20:  V = 8
```

```
410  A = 128
420  B = PEEK(49319)
430  FOR Q = 1 TO 8
440  IF B−A<0 THEN GOTO 500
450  HTAB H: VTAB V: PRINT "ON ";
460  B = B−A
470  A = A/2: V = V+1
480  NEXT Q
490  GOTO 400
500  HTAB H: VTAB V: PRINT "OFF ";
510  GOTO 470
```

When successfully loaded and tested, the program should generate a display such as that shown in Table 6-1. The various ON and OFF conditions shown by your computer will probably be different, based upon the logic switch settings at your input port.

## Step 2

Make notes alongside of Table 6-1 to indicate which bits at the input port correspond to the different labels. You can do this by

**Table 6-1. Control Program Output**

| | |
|---|---|
| ACID PUMP | ON |
| BASE PUMP | OFF |
| HEATER | ON |
| MIXER | ON |
| FLUSH CYCLE | ON |
| DISHWASHER | ON |
| VACUUM | OFF |
| DRYER | OFF |

testing the input bits, or by analyzing your program. You should find that bit D7 is the "ACID PUMP," bit D6 is the "BASE PUMP," and so on, down to bit D0, which is the "DRYER."

## Step 3

Refer to Chapter 4, Example 4-3 and use the Apple monitor to enter this assembly-language program into the computer. You can simply type CALL -151 and then RETURN to enter the monitor. Check that your program has been entered correctly. Remember that the monitor program uses hexadecimal numbers. If you do not know how to use the monitor, refer to *Apple II Reference Manual*, or follow these steps:

1. Press the RESET key and type CALL -151, and press the RETURN key. The Apple should respond with an asterisk ( * ).
2. Type 0300:00 00 00 48 AD 00 03 2D 01 03 8D 02 03 68 60 Leave

a space between the two-digit groups. Use 00 for the first three values in the program.

3. Press the RETURN key, type 02FF, press the RETURN key, then press the RETURN key twice, and check the data against what is in the listing in Example 4-3, and what is noted above.

## Step 4

To test the assembly-language program, enter the program shown below into the computer and run it. Make the necessary decimal-to-binary and binary-to-decimal conversions on scrap paper to check your results. Press RESET to return to BASIC.

```
1000   POKE 10,76:POKE 11,03:POKE 12,03
1010   INPUT "MASK BYTE "; M: POKE 768,M
1020   INPUT "DATA BYTE "; D: POKE 769,D
1030   Q = USR(0): PRINT "ANSWER "; PEEK(770)
1040   GOTO 1010
```

If your answers prove to check with those that you calculate by hand, go on to the next step. If not, carefully check that the assembly-language steps have been entered correctly, and test the program again. Remember, the errors could be in your "hand" calculations.

## Step 5

We now want you to modify your program so that it will detect when *any* of the appliances, DISHWASHER, DRYER, or VACUUM are on, and whenever the ACID PUMP and BASE PUMP are both on. The logical AND assembly-language subroutine can be used, although there are probably other solutions that will also work.

Can you suggest a method of making these determinations? We suggest that you review the logical AND operation, as presented in Chapter 4. Think about the operations as they are presented in Table 6-2.

## Step 6

The logical AND operation can be used to mask out the unwanted bits, D5-D0 for the pump test, and bits D7-D3 for the appliance test. Thus, two "masks" must be established, one for the pumps, and one for the appliances. What would these masks be, in decimal and in binary?

Table 6-2. Control Conditions To Be Detected

| D7 | D6 | D5 | D4 | D3 | D2 | D1 | D0 | |
|----|----|----|----|----|----|----|----|---|
| 1 | 1 | X | X | X | X | X | X | ACID AND BASE PUMPS BOTH ON |
| X | X | X | X | X | 0 | 0 | 1 | |
| X | X | X | X | X | 0 | 1 | 0 | |
| X | X | X | X | X | 0 | 1 | 1 | |
| X | X | X | X | X | 1 | 0 | 0 | ANY APPLIANCE ON |
| X | X | X | X | X | 1 | 0 | 1 | |
| X | X | X | X | X | 1 | 1 | 0 | |
| X | X | X | X | X | 1 | 1 | 1 | |

X = Don't care, logic one or zero.

The mask for the pumps would be $11000000_2$, or 192, while the mask for the appliances would be $00000111_2$, or 7. When these masks are ANDed with the input values from the sensors, or logic switches, the desired bits will be "filtered" through the mask.

**Step 7**

Now that the two masks have been established, suggest some software steps that could be used to determine the state of the "filtered" bits. You need to think of the individual bits, as well as the decimal equivalents for the bits. You may use new variables, if you need to.

We used a new variable, C, to represent the value input from the sensors. This allows the variable B to be used independently in the ON/OFF display portion of the program. If you use the variable B, you will find that it is always zero. We will let you try and find out why. We used either:

```
POKE  768,7:POKE  769:C:Q=USR(0)
IF PEEK(770) = 0 THEN . . .
                or
POKE  768,7:POKE  769,C:Q=USR(0)
IF  PEEK(770) >0 THEN . . .
```

to detect the appliances, and similar steps to detect the pumps. In each case, the THEN . . . statement is executed on one condition, and the program continues on in the other.

## Step 8

In order to test your program ideas, add steps to the basic flag-detecting program so that DANGER is printed on the display if both pumps are on, and APPLIANCES is printed if any of the appliances are on. Write your program steps in the following space and review them carefully before you change the program. Remember that you will need a line just like line 1000 in the program given in Step 4, if you are going to use the assembly-language subroutine. This program line initializes the three locations used by the USR command so that it points the computer to the start of the correct subroutine.

Your program steps will probably look like these:

```
420   B = PEEK(49319): C = B
  .
  .
  .
490   GOTO 600
  .
  .
  .
600   POKE 768,7: POKE 769,C
605   Q = USR(0)
610   IF PEEK(770) = 0 THEN 700
615   HTAB 20:VTAB 17: PRINT "APPLIANCES";
620   POKE 768,192
625   Q = USR(0)
630   IF PEEK(770) <> 192 THEN 800
635   HTAB 20:VTAB 18: PRINT "DANGER";
640   GOTO 400
700   HTAB 20:VTAB 17: PRINT "          ";
710   GOTO 620
800   HTAB 20:VTAB 18: PRINT "          ";
810   GOTO 400
```

Test your program. You may have forgotten steps to clear the AP-PLIANCES and DANGER displays from your screen. You may also have forgotten to use three POKE commands to load the information required by the USR command. You can do this without adding another step to your program, simply type in the POKE commands, followed by a RETURN. They only need to be executed once.

The commands for printing spaces at lines 700 and 800 are used to clear the APPLIANCES and DANGER signals that are displayed. This program could be much more complex, containing steps to use reverse video, or to flash the display when an emergency condition is sensed by the program. You should realize by now that the software can handle both mathematical and logical operations. You should also see that the use of assembly-language subroutines is not too difficult.

You may turn off the computer, although the assembly-language AND operation program will be used again. The input port will also be used again, so do not dismantle your circuit.

## EXPERIMENT NO. 8
## CONSTRUCTING AN OUTPUT PORT

### Purpose

The purpose of this experiment is to have you construct a simple 8-bit output port and investigate its use.

### Discussion

In this experiment, a simple 8-bit latch circuit will be used to construct an output port. The output port will be used in this experiment, and in some of the following experiments, in which it will be necessary to transfer information to external devices. Two SN7475 quad latch integrated circuits will be used.

### Pin Configuration of the Integrated Circuit (Fig. 6-9)

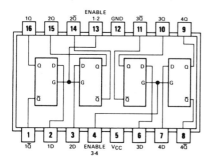

FUNCTION TABLE
(Each Latch)

| INPUTS | | OUTPUTS | |
|---|---|---|---|
| D | G | Q | Q̄ |
| L | H | L | H |
| H | H | H | L |
| X | L | $Q_0$ | $\bar{Q}_0$ |

H = high level, L = low level, X = irrelevant
$Q_0$ = the level of Q before the high-to-low transition of G

**Fig. 6-9. SN7475 4-bit match chip pin configuration.**

## Step 1

The gating circuit used in Experiment No. 2 will be used in this experiment. If this circuit is not available on your solderless breadboard, we suggest that you perform Experiment No. 2 and then this experiment. The gating circuit may also be wired and used directly. Refer to Fig. 6-4 for the circuit details.

## Step 2

Wire the circuit shown in Fig. 6-10. Two SN7475 latch integrated circuits are required, along with eight individual lamp monitors, or

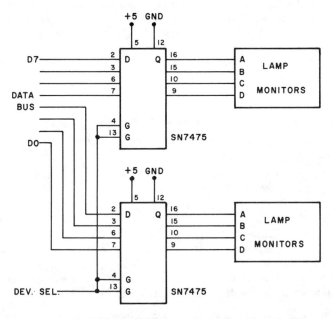

Fig. 6-10. Simple 8-bit output port schematic.

equivalent logic level detecting circuits. Do not connect the device select input, DEV SEL, at this time.

## Step 3

Refer to the circuit shown in Fig. 6-4. Try to determine which of the three control outputs, A, B, or C, would be used to control the latch enable inputs that are connected to the DEV SEL line. Which one would you use? Why?

The A output, $\overline{\text{RD } 49319}$, has already been used and RD 49318 would not work, since it is decoded for an input port. The WR 49318 output (C) would be the choice to use. It provides a positive pulse which is the same type of pulse required by the SN7475 latch chips. This output is also decoded for an output device. You should remember that the $\overline{7}$ and $\overline{6}$ output pins from the decoder on the printed circuit board actually correspond to decoded addresses 49319 and 49318, respectively.

Make a connection between pin 13 on the SN7402 and pins 4 and 13 on both of the SN7475 latch chips. This is the DEV SEL connection shown in Fig. 6-10.

**Step 4**

To test the output port, enter the following program into your computer:

```
10  A = 0
20  POKE 49318,A
30  END
```

Preset the variable A to zero, as shown, and run the program. What happens to the lamp monitors?

They should be unlit, since zero has been transferred to the output port. Now set A to 255 and run the program again. You should see all of the LEDs light. If these conditions have not been found, recheck your circuit and the test program.

**Step 5**

The program may be changed so that you can easily enter new values from the keyboard. The new program is:

```
10  INPUT A
20  POKE  49318,A
30  GOTO 10
```

You may try any values that you choose, but we suggest that you try powers of two first, 0, 1, 2, 4, 8, etc., since these will test the individual LEDs.

Since an 8-bit output port can only display values between zero and 255, what happens when you try to output a value that is outside of this range? Would you expect to see a "portion" of the value, say the eight least-significant bits? Try running the program with the value 256. What happens?

The Apple displays

?ILLEGAL QUANTITY ERROR IN 20

which indicates that the value was not within the proper range for the function that was requested. The line number for the "error" is provided in the error message. Negative numbers are also "caught" in this way.

### Step 6

Restart the program and enter a value of 90. You should observe a display of 01011010 on the lamp monitors. Now try and enter a value of −24. When the error is detected, and the error message displayed, does the displayed value change?

No. Error conditions are detected prior to any attempted use of the POKE function. How do you think the Apple will handle fractional numbers? Enter a decimal fraction, such as 6.01. What is displayed?

The Apple will "strip off" the decimal portion of the number. You may wish to experiment with some other numbers, too.

### Step 7

Can you write a short program that could be used to increment a value from 0 to 255, displaying each new value on the LEDs? Write your program in the space below, and test it. What do you observe? Can you make the program loop back on itself so that the incrementing counting is displayed again and again?

We used the following program:

```
10  FOR A = 0 TO 255
20  POKE 49318,A
30  NEXT A
40  GOTO 10
```

Remember that you cannot go above 255, or below 0, without generating an error message. You may wish to put a short time delay in your program so that the LEDs do not flash on and off so quickly. An example of such a time-delay step is:

```
25  FOR T = 0 TO 500: NEXT T
```

You should see that it is fairly simple to construct an output port, and to control it with simple software commands.

The output port will be used in the following experiment, but the power may be shut off.

### EXPERIMENT NO. 9
### OUTPUT-PORT AND INPUT-PORT INTERACTIONS

**Purpose**

The purpose of this experiment is to show you how input-port and output-port commands can be used in the same program.

**Discussion**

In many cases, input ports and output ports will be used together in interface circuits. They will be controlled by PEEK and POKE commands within the same program, and there frequently will be transfers of information between the ports. In this experiment, you will observe how such ports may be used together in a simple circuit.

**Step 1**

The simple input port (Experiment No. 7) and output port (Experiment No. 8) used previously will be used in this experiment. We refer you to Experiment Nos. 2, 3, and 8 for the appropriate circuit details.

**Step 2**

Once the input port and output port have been constructed, enter the following program into your computer and run it. It is used to test the I/O port circuits.

```
10  A = PEEK(49319)
20  POKE 49318,A
30  GOTO 10
```

As you actuate the logic switches at the input port, you should see the corresponding bits at the output port change, consistent with the switch actions. If this is not the case, recheck your circuits and your program.

**Step 3**

In this step, two values will be entered from the keyboard and then displayed on the LEDs. At this point, you should be able to write a short program to do this. Make an attempt in the space provided:

We used the following program, in which a most-significant byte (MSBY) and a least-significant byte (LSBY) were simulated:

```
10    INPUT "MSBY ";A$: M = PEEK(49319)
20    INPUT "LSBY ";A$: L = PEEK(49319)
30    POKE 49318,M
40    INPUT A$
50    POKE 49318,L
60    GOTO 10
```

In this program, the string variable, A$, has been used as a "dummy" variable to "stop" the computer so that you can perform the necessary actions before the program goes on.

**Step 4**

Run your program. You should be able to enter two values into the computer. When you type RUN RETURN, the computer is ready for you to set the MSBY on the switches. After you have done this, press the RETURN key, so that the computer can perform the data acquisition step. Then, set the LSBY on the switches and again press RETURN. When the LSBY has been acquired, the MSBY will be displayed. By pressing RETURN, you will cause the computer to display the LSBY.

**Step 5**

This program shows how the computer can acquire and store values for later display. Eight bits of information are easy to manipulate. How could a number between 0 and 65535 be displayed on two output ports?

These numbers would have to be "split" into an 8-bit MSBY and an 8-bit LSBY. Can you suggest how this might be done?

The number could be divided by 256 to get the MSBY as the *integer* portion of the answer. For example, if we start with the number 10923:

10923/256 = 42.668

The integer portion of the result, 42, when converted into an 8-bit binary number, would be the MSBY of the value. The LSBY can also be calculated:

10923 − (42 ∗ 256) = 171

Here, the 171 must also be converted into its 8-bit binary equivalent to be the LSBY.

A BASIC program can be written for the Apple to perform these functions. Could you write it?

### Step 6

We developed the following program to make the "conversion:"

```
10   INPUT "VALUE "; V
20   M = V/256
30   L = V − INT(M) ∗ 256
40   PRINT INT(M), L
50   INPUT A$
60   POKE 49318,M
70   INPUT A$
80   POKE 49318,L
90   GOTO 10
```

The MSBY and the LSBY will be displayed on the video monitor in their decimal form. The INT command has been used to "strip" the decimal fraction from the value for M, for clarity. This is not required for the POKE operation, since the decimal fraction will be ignored.

## Step 7

Enter our program, or yours, into the computer and test it. You will have to press the RETURN key to display the MSBY on the LEDs, and you must press it a second time to display the LSBY.

Can you enter values greater than 65535? Can they be converted and displayed?

Yes, you can enter them, and they will be converted, but you cannot display them, since they will generate results that are greater than 256 in the MSBY. This generates an error condition. Can you do anything to prevent this?

You can add some steps to your program that will check the range of the value before attempting the conversion. Steps can also be added to remove any fractional portions of the number. The following steps can be used:

```
12  IF V < = 65535 AND V > = 0 THEN 18
14  PRINT "VALUE OUT OF RANGE, TRY AGAIN": GOTO 10
18  V = INT(V)
```

You might want to try adding these steps to your program. Program steps such as these prevent errors, and they orient the program toward the user. Keep this type of programming in mind when you write complex programs of your own.

### EXPERIMENT NO. 10
### DATA LOGGING AND DISPLAY

#### Purpose

The purpose of this experiment is to show you how the input port may be used to acquire information, and how the computer can store this information for later display at the LEDs.

#### Discussion

In this experiment, a set of 10 data values will be acquired from the three-state input port, and will be displayed on the LEDs at a later time. More flexible display ideas will also be developed and larger lists of data acquired.

## Step 1

The input port and output port described previously will be used in this experiment. By now, you should be familiar with these types of ports, but we refer you to Experiment Nos. 2, 3, and 8 for the necessary details. If you have not performed these experiments, we recommend that you do so before going on with this experiment.

## Step 2

In this experiment, you will use the computer to acquire and display a set of values that are acquired from the input port. While these may be acquired with software steps such as:

```
50   INPUT A$
60   Q = PEEK(49319)
70   INPUT A$
80   R = PEEK(49319)
```

this takes a great number of software steps to acquire a small amount of information. Can you suggest an alternative?

A list of values can be acquired by using a loop, and an array can be used to store the information, so that a new variable need not be assigned to each new data value. Can you write a short program that could be used to acquire 10 data points?

We used the following program, which should look somewhat like yours. Note the use of an array to store the information.

```
10   DIM A(10)
20   PRINT "START"
30   FOR P = 1 TO 10
40   INPUT A$
50   A(P) = PEEK(49319)
60   NEXT P
70   PRINT "START DISPLAY. . ."
```

```
80    FOR P = 1 TO 10
90    GET A$
100   PRINT A(P): POKE 49318,A(P)
110   NEXT P
120   PRINT "END OF RUN": END
```

In this program, you must press the RETURN key to cause the computer to acquire a value. When the computer prints "START DISPLAY..." on the screen, it will display a value that it has stored, each time you press RETURN. The value will also be displayed on the LEDs in binary form. Note that a GET A$ command has been used here, instead of an INPUT A$. Is there any difference?

Yes, the GET A$ command suppresses the question mark (?), and any character key (A, &, 1, etc.) may be used in place of the RE-TURN key. The alphanumeric symbol *is not* displayed. This "cleans up" the display of the data values.

**Step 3**

Run either your program, or ours, to acquire 10 data values. Once the values have been acquired, use the computer to display them. What results do you observe?

You should find that your values have been stored properly, and that they are also displayed and printed on the video monitor. If you do not require the values at the output port, could you modify the program so that it only displays the values on the monitor?

Yes. Simply change line 100 to:

```
100   PRINT A(P)
```

and remove line 90.

**Step 4**

The low-resolution graphics mode on the Apple could also be used to display the values in graphical form. We suggest that you attempt to use the HLIN command to draw a horizontal set of lines that represent the relative values that have been input from the port. Remember that there are limits on the dimensions of the screen area for the HLIN command. These limits are 39 points in each direction.

Note your display program steps in the following space:

We used the following steps to generate a horizontal bar graph of the information:

```
 80   GR: COLOR = 5
 90   FOR P = 1 TO 10
100   D = A(P)/6.5
110   HLIN 0,D AT P
120   NEXT P
130   END
```

These steps were added to the program that we developed in Step 2. Try your program, or the one shown here.

In this set of program steps, the data value has been divided by 6.5, so that instead of having a range between 0 and 255, the range is "condensed" to be 0 to 39. The subscript for the array has also been used to increase the starting position of each horizontal line. The data starts at the top of the screen for $A(1)$, and proceeds down the screen for the later data values. You could also use the value of P to change the color for each of the horizontal lines.

## Step 5

Additional changes can be made to the program so that a time-delay routine is used in place of the INPUT A$ command. This would mean that data values would be obtained at definite intervals, as programmed in the delay routine. You would no longer need to press the RETURN key to have a new data value acquired.

Change your program so that a time delay routine is used in place of the INPUT A$ command at line 40. Make the delay fairly long, about 2 or 3 seconds. Here is an example of a useful routine:

```
40   FOR T = 0 to 2000: NEXT T
```

Connect the logic probe to the "A" output, pin 1, on the SN7402 NOR gate. The acquisition of a data value from the three-state input port will cause the logic probe to flash the yellow LED. This will tell you that a value has been acquired.

You may want to change your program to acquire more than 10 points. With the simple display routine, you can acquire up to 39 values.

Make the necessary changes to your program so that a time delay is used to synchronize the acquisition of the data from the input port. Run your program. You may want to increase the delay so that you can easily change the switches.

Your program should now look something like this:

```
10   DIM A(10)
20   PRINT "START"
30   FOR P = 1 TO 10
40   FOR T = 0 TO 2000: NEXT T
50   A(P) = PEEK(49319)
60   NEXT P
70   PRINT "START DISPLAY. . ."
80   GR: COLOR = 5
90   FOR P = 1 TO 10
100  D = A(P)/6.5
110  HLIN 0,D AT P
120  NEXT P
130  END
```

Have you noticed that not all of your values cause changes in the display? Try entering values of 0, 1, 2, 3, and so on up to 9. You may need to slow down the delay, or to go back to the INPUT A$ command at line 40 so that you have sufficient time to make the changes to the switches. What do you find in the display when you enter these numbers? Why?

The values 0-6 show the same value on the display, and the values 7-9 also show the same value, but one "square" greater than the previous values, 0-6. The reason for this is that all the values are "compressed" to be between 0 and 39, so the resolution is cut from one-part-in-256 to one-part-in-40. Thus while the data has 256 discrete values, the display only can accommodate 40 different values. The division of the value by 6.5 "compresses" it to fit in the space available on the display. You will also note that a value of zero still "lights" one square on the video monitor. Unfortunately, the BASIC program will generate one "lit" square for the command HLIN 0,0 at X, wherever X is on the screen.

The point of this experiment is that the computer can be used to acquire information and display it, or use it, in many ways. The input and output ports are simply additional ways of getting information into and out of the computer.

## EXPERIMENT NO. 11
## SIMPLE DIGITAL-TO-ANALOG CONVERTER

### Purpose

The purpose of this experiment is to show you how a simple 8-bit digital-to-analog converter (DAC or D/A) can be interfaced to the Apple.

### Discussion

A simple D/A converter, the Signetics NE5018 8-bit converter, will be interfaced to the Apple. Although we have not discussed analog converters, they have been thoroughly described in *Micro-computer-Analog Converter Software and Hardware Interfacing* (Howard W. Sams & Co., Inc., Indianapolis, IN 46268). We refer you to this book for additional information about these devices. Other topics, such as sample and hold amplifiers, analog multiplexers and instrumentation amplifiers are also described.

### Pin Configuration of the Integrated Circuit (Fig. 6-11)

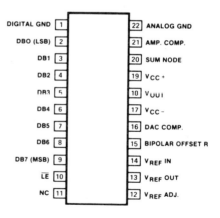

Fig. 6-11. Signetics NE5018 8-bit D/A converter chip pin configuration.

| | | |
|---|---|---|
| DIGITAL GND | 1 | 22 ANALOG GND |
| DB0 (LSB) | 2 | 21 AMP. COMP. |
| DB1 | 3 | 20 SUM NODE |
| DB2 | 4 | 19 $V_{CC}+$ |
| DB3 | 5 | 18 $V_{OUT}$ |
| DB4 | 6 | 17 $V_{CC}-$ |
| DB5 | 7 | 16 DAC COMP. |
| DB6 | 8 | 15 BIPOLAR OFFSET R |
| DB7 (MSB) | 9 | 14 $V_{REF}$ IN |
| $\overline{LE}$ | 10 | 13 $V_{REF}$ OUT |
| NC | 11 | 12 $V_{REF}$ ADJ. |

### Step 1

Two additional power supplies are required in this experiment, $+12$ and $-12$ volts. They will be used to power the D/A converter integrated circuit. Be sure that these power supplies are available, and that they are adjusted for the proper voltages before proceeding.

Wire the circuit shown in Fig. 6-12. The device-select pulse is obtained from the SN7402 NOR gate circuit that has been used in previous experiments. The device-select signal is available from

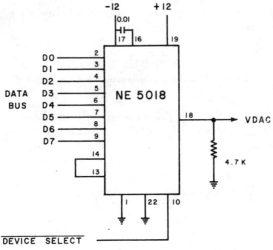

Fig. 6-12. Schematic for simple D/A converter interface, using NE5018 D/A converter chip.

point C (Fig. 6-4), but it must be inverted before it can be used by the NE5018 chip. An SN7404 inverter chip may be used for this, as shown in Fig. 6-13. Wire this inverter circuit, too, connecting the input of the SN7404 inverter to pin 13 on the SN7402, and wiring the output of the SN7404 inverter to the DEVICE SELECT input on the NE5018 converter.

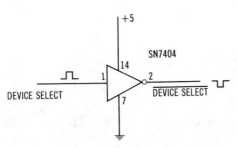

Fig. 6-13. Simple device-select pulse-inverter circuit.

At this point, carefully check the +12 and −12-volt power supply connections to be sure that they are correct. If you are using separate power supplies, you must be sure that there is a low-resistance ground connection in common to all of them and to the breadboard.

## Step 2

The NE5018 D/A converter will convert values between 0 and 255 to voltages between 0 and +10 volts. Since the 0- to 10-volt range has been divided into 256 values, or 255 steps, the voltage increment available is:

$$10 \text{ volts}/255 \text{ steps} = 39 \text{ millivolts/step}$$

You can probably write a short program that would increment an 8-bit count and output it to the DA converter. Don't worry about the internal operation of the D/A converter, just treat it like an output port. Your program will generate a slowly increasing positive voltage ramp. Develop your program in the space below:

We used the program:

```
10   FOR  V  =  0  TO  255
20   POKE  43918,V
30   NEXT  V
40   GOTO  10
```

A simple voltmeter or volt-ohm-milliammeter (vom) may be used to monitor the voltages. Connect the meter between ground and the NE5018 VDAC output (VDAC is positive). Try your program. Does the voltage increase slowly? What happens when the voltage reaches about +10 volts?

The voltage increases slowly to +10 volts. When it reaches this value, it quickly changes to zero volts, or ground, and it starts to increase slowly once again.

You can slow the voltage ramp by introducing a short time delay routine in your program. We used the following:

```
25   FOR  T  =  0  TO  100:  NEXT  T
```

**Step 3**

Develop a program that will generate a negative-going ramp, and one that will generate a triangular ramp (slow-up then slow-down).

We used the following programs:

**Negative ramp**
```
10   FOR  V  =  255  TO  0  STEP  −1
```

```
20   POKE 49318, V
30   NEXT V
40   GOTO 10
```
**Triangular output**
```
10   FOR V = 0 TO 255
20   POKE 49318, V
30   NEXT V
40   FOR V = 254 TO 1 STEP −1
50   POKE  49318, V
60   NEXT V
70   GOTO 10
```

You may wish to try either of these programs, or the ones that you wrote. Why is the range in one of the triangular output loops 254 to 1 instead of 255 to 0?

If the range is 255 to 0, these two values will be output twice, although you probably couldn't tell the difference on the meter. A time delay, or delays, may be useful in these programs.

## Step 4

Since you know that the voltage from 0 to 10 volts corresponds to steps from 0 to 255, can you write a program that would allow you to enter a voltage from the keyboard and that would generate this voltage on the meter? Use the following space for your program:

We developed the following program, which you may wish to try:

```
10   INPUT "VOLTAGE ";V
20   R = V * 25.5
30   POKE 49318, R
40   GOTO 10
```

## Step 5

Try your program, too. Does it generate a voltage from the D/A converter that closely matches the voltage that you entered? Our program seemed to work well, considering inaccuracies in the meter. This program does not have any "error detecting" steps, so you can also try and generate a +15-volt signal from the converter. What do you think will happen? Will the converter burn out?

The converter will not burn out, since it can only accept an 8-bit value, which corresponds to an output of +10 volts. The "15" input for 15 volts will cause an ILLEGAL QUANTITY ERROR, since we are trying to transfer the value 382 to an 8-bit device. It just can't be done with eight bits.

**Step 6**

At this point, you should be able to write a program that will allow you to enter an upper voltage and a lower voltage, and to have the Apple generate a triangular wave between them. Use your best programming skills.

We used the following program:

```
10   INPUT "UPPER VOLTAGE"; H
20   IF H <= 10 AND H >= 0 THEN 40
30   PRINT "VOLTAGE OUT OF BOUNDS": GOTO 10
40   INPUT "LOWER VOLTAGE"; L
50   IF L <= 10 AND L >= 0
60   PRINT "VOLTAGE OUT OF BOUNDS": GOTO 40
70   IF H > L THEN 90
80   PRINT "UPPER V MUST BE HIGHER THAN LOWER V": GOTO 10
90   H = H * 25.5: L = L * 25.5
100  FOR V = L TO H
110  POKE 49318, V
120  NEXT V
130  FOR V = H-1 TO L+1 STEP -1
140  POKE 49318, V
150  NEXT V
160  GOTO 100
```

Run your program and test it. You should be able to make the meter needle "swing" between the upper and lower voltages. You may use a time delay, or delays, if you wish to slow the meter movement so that you can easily watch it.

This experiment clearly shows you how a simple D/A converter may be interfaced to your computer. The NE5018 used internal latches, and much of the analog circuitry has been placed on the converter chip. D/A converters find use in applications that require the computer to control voltage-dependent devices, such as servo motors, amplifiers, etc.

You will not use the NE5018 D/A converter again, so you may remove it from your breadboard. The SN7402 NOR gate chip should be retained, but the SN7404 inverter may be removed. Power may be turned off. Carefully remove the connections to the +12- and

−12-volt power supplies, so that they will not come in contact with any of the circuits.

## EXPERIMENT NO. 12
## OUTPUT PORTS, BCD, AND BINARY CODES

### Purpose

The purpose of this experiment is to explore the use of an SN74-LS373 chip as an output port.

### Discussion

Newer integrated circuits, such as the SN74LS373 octal latch, are available to simplify the task of output-port construction. In this experiment, you will construct an 8-bit output port using one of these chips, and the use of binary-coded decimal numbers will be explored.

### Pin Configuration of the Integrated Circuit (Fig. 6-14)

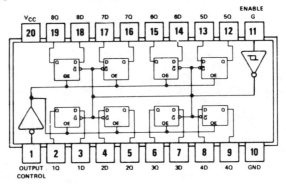

Fig. 6-14. SN74LS373 octal latch chip pin configuration.

### Step 1

Wire the circuit shown in Fig. 6-15. You may use output "C," pin 13, on the NOR gate circuit shown in Fig. 6-4 as the "G" input to the SN74LS373 chip. If this NOR gate circuit is not wired on your breadboard, refer to Experiment No. 2.

### Step 2

Note that the SN74LS373 chip has two control inputs, G and OC. The G input controls the latch, and the OC input controls the latch outputs, which are three-state. Thus, the latch may be used not only to obtain information from a bus, but to pass it on to another bus, as well. The relationships of the signals are shown in Table 6-3.

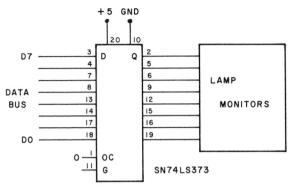

**Fig. 6-15. Using SN74LS373 octal latch chip as output port.**

**Table 6-3. Control Signal Truth Table for the SN74LS373**

| Output Control | Enable (G) | Data | Output |
|----------------|------------|------|--------|
| L | H | H | H |
| L | H | L | L |
| L | L | X | Qo |
| H | X | X | Z |

When the Output Control (OC) signal is a logic one, the outputs have been disabled, or placed in the high-impedance state (HI-Z). When the enable or Gating input (G) is a logic one, the information present at the D inputs is passed through the latch circuits to the Q outputs. This is the same type of operation that was observed for the SN7475 latch chip.

In this experiment, the OC input should be grounded (logic zero), so that the outputs arc always enabled.

**Step 3**

Once the output port has been wired, test it by writing a short program that will take values from the keyboard and display them in binary at the output port. A binary incrementing-count program can also be used to test the port. You should be able to write programs such as these without any further assistance.

**Step 4**

Enter the following program into your computer and run it.

```
10  FOR C = 0 TO 255
20  POKE 49318, C
30  FOR T = 0 TO 500: NEXT T
40  NEXT C
50  GOTO 10
```

What do you observe at the LEDs?

You should see a slowly incrementing binary count. You may increase the length of the time delay at line 30, if you wish.

Now that the LEDs are displaying an increasing binary count, carefully remove the connection between the OC pin, pin 1, on the SN74LS373 chip and ground. What happens to the display, or LEDs? When you replace this connection, what do you observe?

In our set of LEDs, all of the LEDs became unlit when the connection was removed. When the OC input pin was again grounded, the count was found to be continuing. *The Output Control signal did not affect the count.* Even though the outputs were disabled and placed into their high-impedance state, the counting continued, and the latches were "updated" with new information by the computer. In our system, the high-impedance state of the outputs caused the LEDs to be turned off. This may be different from your observations, but you should see that the latch outputs change dramatically when the OC input pin is not at ground.

The SN74LS373 chip is called a three-state octal latch chip, since it has three-state outputs on eight latch functions. This chip is particularly useful in computer interface circuits, since it contains all eight latches, and since its outputs may be placed in the high-impedance state. The SN74LS373 can be used in complex interfaces that are connected to several different computer buses. In fact, the SN74LS373 could be used as part of a communication circuit that could link two or more computers.

**Step 5**

Now that you have another input port wired on your breadboard, we will use it to further explore some of the manipulations that can be performed by the Apple. In past examples, we have used the computer to control an incrementing *binary* count. This is not the only code that is in digital electronic equipment. Another popular code is the binary-coded decimal format, in which decimal digits are each assigned their own binary code, independent of the other digits. Of course, this code is still "binary," in the sense that only two states are possible for each bit. For example, the decimal number 9530 would be represented as 1001 0101 0011 0000 in binary-coded decimal, or bcd. Note the separation between each set of four bits. One set of four bits is used to represent the decimal digit for each decade. The bcd code is used in many electronic devices, and is used to control seven-segment displays and other decimally oriented devices.

We would like you to try and write a program that will "split" a number into its bcd equivalents. The output port will be used to display the different groups, two bcd digits at a time. The ten's and one's bcd digits should be displayed at the output port first, followed by the thousand's and hundred's bcd digits. You may use the RE-TURN, or other key to "stop" the computer between displays of the digits.

We used the following program:

```
10   INPUT "VALUE "; A
20   IF A < 10000 THEN 30 ELSE 10
30   GOSUB 1000
40   POKE 49318, A+C
50   GET A$:A = B
60   GOSUB 1000
70   POKE 49318, A+C
80   GOTO 10

1000  B = 0: C = 0
1010  IF A > 99 THEN 1100
1020  IF A < 10 THEN RETURN
1030  C = C+16: A = A−10
1040  GOTO 1020
1100  A = A−100: B = B+1
1110  GOTO 1010
```

In the subroutine, the variables are A, B, and C. In this case, the A represents the decimal value to be converted to bcd (the starting value), B represents the "hundreds," while C represents the "tens."

At the end of the subroutine, A represents the units, or "ones." You could have used a new variable for this purpose, if you wished.

In some cases, it may be difficult for you to remember that you are tricking the Apple into generating bcd values for you, since you are really interested in the *binary codes* that are being output to the port. Thus, while you have tricked the Apple into outputting the binary pattern 10011001, which represents 99 in bcd, the Apple really thinks that it is outputting a decimal 153, which is the number that causes the binary pattern, 10011001, to appear on the LEDs. There are many different ways in which you can "fool" the computer into working with odd codes, or codes that do not match the ones that it normally uses.

If you are going to go on to further experiments, you may want to leave the SN74LS373 output port on your breadboard. However, if you already have another output port already available, the SN-74LS373 circuit may be removed. Power may be turned off.

## EXPERIMENT NO. 13
## OUTPUT-PORTS TRAFFIC-LIGHT CONTROLLER

### Purpose

The purpose of this experiment is to show you how the Apple computer may be used as a controller in a real application.

### Discussion

While the control of a traffic light may not seem like a realistic problem for us to tackle with the computer, it does illustrate the ability of the computer to make decisions and control external events.

### Step 1

An 8-bit output port will be used in this experiment. If you have one already connected to your computer, you can use it as long as it can control some LEDs. If you have completed one of the output port experiments, you may use one of the output port circuits used in the experiment. If you need to construct an output port, we refer you to Experiment No. 8.

Lamp monitors or individual LEDs may be used to simulate the lamps of the traffic light. Only six LEDs are needed, since the north-south and east-west lamps would be the same, with a red, yellow, and green lamp for each. We used colored LEDs and we adopted the following convention:

| BIT | LED | | BIT | LED | |
|-----|-----|---|-----|-----|---|
| D0 | RED | ⎫ | D3 | RED | ⎫ |
| D1 | YELLOW | ⎬ ELM | D4 | YELLOW | ⎬ MAIN |
| D2 | GREEN | ⎭ | D5 | GREEN | ⎭ |

## Step 2

You must now determine the patterns of logic ones and zeros that are required to turn the individual LEDs on or off. In our circuit, the latch chips were used to drive the LEDs directly, and a zero turned a LED on, while a one turned a LED off. What values are you going to use to turn the various LEDs on and off?

We found that the following binary values were needed. The decimal equivalents have also been provided for you.

| | | | | | | | |
|-----|--------|-----|----------|------|--------|-----|----------|
| ELM | Red | 254 | 11111110 | MAIN | Red | 247 | 11110111 |
| ELM | Yellow | 253 | 11111101 | MAIN | Yellow | 239 | 11101111 |
| ELM | Green | 251 | 11111011 | MAIN | Green | 223 | 11011111 |

## Step 3

To start the traffic-light control operation, write a program that will flash the yellow light on Main Street and the red light on Elm Street; one second on and one second off. What is the "on" pattern, and what is the "off" pattern?

The off pattern is 255, or all logic ones, while the on pattern has bits D4 and D0 both as logic zeros, or $238_{10}$. We used the following program:

```
10   POKE 49318,255
20   FOR T = 0 TO 770: NEXT T
30   POKE 49318,238
40   FOR T = 0 TO 770: NEXT T
50   GOTO 10
```

## Step 4

Determine the lamp patterns that will be required for normal traffic light operation. How many are used? What are they? How can they be stored in the computer?

There are only four patterns. They are (a) red on Elm, green on Main (222), (b) red on Elm, yellow on Main (238), (c) green on Elm, red on Main (243), and (d) yellow on Elm, red on Main (245). The values could be stored through the use of DATA statements, subscripted variables, or just as variables, one per lamp pattern.

## Step 5

In the remainder of this experiment, we will assume a "yellow period" of two seconds. Thus, if Elm Street is on a 10-second period, the green light will be on for 10 seconds, followed by a 2-second yellow, before the signal goes to red.

Write a program that will allow you to sequence through the light patterns, with a 6-second period on Elm and a 10-second period on Main Street.

We used the following program:

```
10  M = 10: E = 6: P =  49318
20  DATA 222, 238, 243, 245
30  READ L
40  POKE P,L
50  FOR R = 1 TO M
```

```
 60   FOR T = 0 TO 770: NEXT T
 70   NEXT R
 80   READ L
 90   POKE P,L
100   GOSUB 1000
110   READ L
120   POKE P,L
130   FOR R = 1 TO E
140   FOR T = 0 TO 770: NEXT T
150   NEXT R
160   READ L
170   POKE P,L
180   GOSUB 1000
190   RESTORE
200   GOTO 30

1000  FOR R = 1 TO 2
1010  FOR T = 0 TO 770: NEXT T
1020  NEXT R
1030  RETURN
```

## Step 6

While the program listed in the previous step will operate correctly, many of the steps are repetitive. Could you suggest a new program that could be written in a simpler way? How would you simplify the program?

In the program in Step 5, the only changes in the four basic sections of the program are to the time delays and the light patterns. By using an array of values, one simple loop may be used. We found that the following program worked well:

```
 10   A(1) = 222: A(2) = 238: A(3) = 243: A(4) = 245
 20   M(1) = 0: M(2) = 2: M(3) = 0: M(4) = 2
 30   INPUT "MAIN DELAY "; M(1)
 40   INPUT "ELM DELAY "; M(3)
 50   FOR Q = 1 TO 4
 60   POKE 49318, A(Q)
 70   FOR R = 1 TO M(Q)
 80   FOR T = 0 TO 770: NEXT T
 90   NEXT R
100   NEXT Q
110   GOTO 50
```

In this new program, the A array stores the light patterns, while the M array stores the time intervals.

## Step 7

So far, the computer has served only as a sequencer, generating the proper lamp patterns and time delays. In this step, some control steps will be added to the traffic-light control program.

The traffic on Main Street is usually heavy, so the normal mode for the traffic light should be green on Main and red on Elm. The program should be able to detect a single car waiting on Elm, so that it may be given the green light. However, Main Street must be given at least 30 seconds of "green time," before any cars are sensed on Elm Street. This means that every car waiting on Elm Street will not automatically trigger a green-on-Elm sequence. To make things even more interesting, there is a sensor on Main Street, too. If five or more cars are waiting on Main Street at a red light, Main Street will be given the green light, and the cars on Elm will have to wait.

In order to program this, you may wish to draw a simple flowchart of the problem. An input port could be used to simulate the two road sensors, but to teach you a bit more about the Apple, the keyboard will be used instead.

The keyboard uses two memory addresses for control. Address 49152 contains the keyboard data, and address 49168 is used as a flag-clear pulse output.

Enter the following program into your computer and run it:

```
2000  PRINT PEEK(49152): GOTO 2000
```

Press some of the keys on the keyboard and note what happens on the display. What do you observe?

There is a new decimal value displayed whenever a new key is pressed, and the value continues to be displayed until a new key is actuated. Thus, the information at input port 49152 represents the code of the *last key* that was pressed.

## Step 8

We would like to have the computer input a value from the keyboard input port only when a key has been pressed. To do this, you must use the keyboard flag bit, which is bit D7 at input port 49152. If this bit is a logic zero, all values from this port will be less than 128. If this bit is a logic one, the values will be 128 or greater, up to 255.

Thus, by testing the value input from the input port, you can determine if a key has been pressed. Of course, after a key is "detected," you must reset the flag bit, with a read operation to address 49168.

Enter the following program into your computer and run it:

```
2000   IF PEEK(49152) >= 128 THEN PRINT PEEK(49152)
2010   Z = PEEK(49168)
2020   GOTO 2000
```

Now press some of the keys, one at a time. What is displayed? Is the decimal code for each key displayed as you press it?

You have probably found that some keys are "missed," once in a while. Since the keyboard flag is cleared during every pass through the loop, it is possible to have the Apple clear a keyboard flag before it is detected. You would really want to have the flag cleared only *after* a key has been detected.

**Step 9**

Write a short keyboard control program that will detect every key, only once, and print its decimal equivalent.

We used the following program that constantly checked the keyboard, but which only printed a character when the flag was set, and only then cleared the keyboard flag.

```
2000   IF PEEK(49152) < 128 GOTO 2000
2010   PRINT PEEK(49152)
2020   Z = PEEK(49168)
2030   GOTO 2000
```

Note that the variable, Z, is a dummy variable, provided simply so that the keyboard flag may be cleared with the PEEK(49168) command.

If you want to use the decimal value for a key, without the flag bit, simply subtract 128.

**Step 10**

Write your traffic-light controller program and test it, using the "E" key as the Elm Street sensor, and the "M" key as the Main Street sensor. Of course, you will have to determine the corresponding key codes.

We used approximately 10-second periods, for test purposes, with 2-second yellow periods. The program that we used is listed for you:

```
10   A = 0: P = 49318
20   POKE P, 222
30   FOR R = 0 TO 10
40   FOR T = 0 TO 770: NEXT T
50   NEXT R
55   Z = PEEK(49168)
60   IF PEEK(49152) = 197 GOTO 80
70   GOTO 60
80   Z = PEEK(49168): POKE P, 238
90   FOR R = 1 TO 2
100  FOR T = 0 TO 770: NEXT T
110  NEXT R
120  POKE P, 243
130  FOR R = 0 TO 1000
150  IF PEEK(49152) = 205 THEN 190
170  NEXT R
180  GOTO 210
190  Z = PEEK(49168): A = A+1
200  IF A < 5 THEN 170
210  POKE P, 245
220  FOR R = 1 TO 2
230  FOR T = 0 TO 770: NEXT T
240  NEXT R
250  GOTO 10
```

You should note that the keyboard flag is reset before it is tested at line 60. This clears any keyboard entries that are made during the first 10-second period. You can remove this step, if you want the Elm Street sensor to "remember" any cars that trip it during this period.

The flag-detecting step at line 150 has been embedded in the overall timing loop. This means that the flag is always being checked, and that these flag-detecting steps must be figured into the overall delay period. You can do this by testing various values of the delay constant at line 130.

There are many other things that this program could do. For example, many intersections have pedestrian control signals, left-hand turn signals, flashing lights, and other special features. You could make the program as complex as you wish. In this situation, the timing is not particularly critical. It wouldn't really matter if the cars had to wait an extra second or two while a flag is tested. However, periods of 10 or 20 seconds could be annoying to drivers. Keep this in mind as you program. In some cases, the time requirements will be so strict, and the time periods so short, that assembly-language programming is dictated.

The six LEDs should be removed from the breadboard, but the output port should be retained, since you will use it in the next experiment. Power may be turned off.

## EXPERIMENT NO. 14
## LOGIC-DEVICE TESTER

### Purpose

The purpose of this experiment is to show you how the computer can be used to test an electronic device. In this case, simple gates are used.

### Discussion

Most logic chips that contain gates may be tested by applying known logic levels to their inputs and then comparing the outputs with the truth-table for the device being tested. In this experiment, the computer will be used in such a manner. One input port and one output port are required. Various devices, such as SN7400, SN7402, SN7408, etc., may be tested. The test is a functional test, and not a test for dynamic properties, such as switching time, propagation delay, and other parameters.

### Step 1

You will need to construct an input port and an output port for use in this experiment. You should be able to construct such ports without further assistance. Many of the previous experiments have detailed this for you. You may wish to use an SN74LS373 chip as

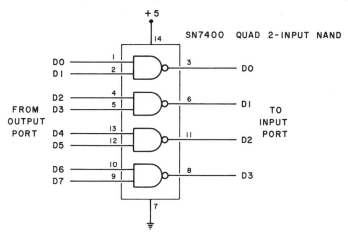

Fig. 6-16. Schematic for the SN7400 NAND gate test circuit.

the input port. When these ports have been constructed and tested, go on to the next step.

## Step 2

The test configuration for an SN7400 NAND-gate package is shown in Fig. 6-16. For the pin configuration of other chips, we refer you to Fig. 6-17.

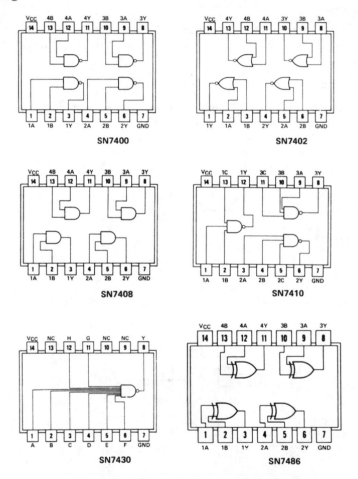

Fig. 6-17. Pin configurations of some standard gates.

Wire the test circuit as shown in Fig. 6-16. Remember to connect the +5-volt and ground inputs to both the interface chips and to the circuit that is to be tested. The unused inputs at the input port should be grounded.

You should be able to develop the truth tables for the various gates shown in Fig. 6-17, starting with the NAND gate. For a two-input gate, there are only four combinations of inputs. How many combinations would there be for four gates in a single integrated circuit package?

Possibly you said 16 combinations, four for each of the four gates, or 256 combinations, the number possible with eight binary inputs. Actually, there are only four meaningful combinations, since all of the gates are tested at the same time. Knowing that one gate is bad for one particular combination of inputs does not serve much purpose. If one gate is bad, then the entire "package" is bad.

## Step 3

What are the four combinations of eight bits that will be used at the output port to test the NAND gate? You should write down both the decimal and binary values for these numbers.

Our values were:

| | | | | |
|---|---|---|---|---|
| 00 | 00 | 00 | 00 | = 0 |
| 01 | 01 | 01 | 01 | = 85 |
| 10 | 10 | 10 | 10 | = 170 |
| 11 | 11 | 11 | 11 | = 255 |

Since the outputs have been connected to input bits D3-D0, we would expect them to be all ones or all zeros, that is 0 or 15, depending upon the test pattern. To "remove" the unused bits, D7-D4, we have grounded them. What will they be when they are input? Will this affect the results? Can you suggest another way of "removing" these bits from the test data?

The bits will be input as logic zeros, and they should not affect the data. If the bits are not grounded, a logical AND operation could be used to mask them. The assembly-language subroutine could be used.

## Step 4

Develop a short program that will test the NAND gate that you have interfaced. Your program may closely resemble the traffic-light control program shown in Experiment No. 13, Step 6. The program does not have to be very complex.

The following program worked quite well in this application:

```
10   T(1) = 0: T(2) = 85: T(3) = 170: T(4) = 255
20   R(1) = 15: R(2) = 15: R(3) =15: R(4) =0
30   FOR S =1 TO 4
40   POKE 49318, T(S)
50   IF PEEK(49319) <> R(S) THEN 100
60   NEXT S
70   PRINT "TEST OK": END
100  PRINT "FAILURE": END
```

**Step 5**

Since the pin configurations for the SN7400, SN7408 and SN7486 are equivalent, that is, inputs and outputs are at the same positions on the chips, could a generalized test program be developed for them? How?

Yes, a generalized test program could be developed so that the user could enter the device name, while the computer set up the appropriate truth-table information to be used in the tests. The truth tables are provided in Table 6-4.

You should note that the test patterns are all the same, only the results change.

We used the following test program:

Table 6-4. Truth Tables for the NAND, AND, and EXOR Gates

| SN7400 | | | SN7408 | | | SN7486 | | |
|---|---|---|---|---|---|---|---|---|
| A | B | OUT | A | B | OUT | A | B | OUT |
| 0 | 0 | 1 | 0 | 0 | 0 | 0 | 0 | 0 |
| 0 | 1 | 1 | 0 | 1 | 0 | 0 | 1 | 1 |
| 1 | 0 | 1 | 1 | 0 | 0 | 1 | 0 | 1 |
| 1 | 1 | 0 | 1 | 1 | 1 | 1 | 1 | 0 |

```
10   INPUT "LAST TWO DIGITS ";A$
20   IF A$ = "00" THEN 200
30   IF A$ = "08" THEN 300
40   IF A$ = "86" THEN 400
50   PRINT "TEST NOT AVAILABLE": GOTO 10
60   T(1) = 0: T(2) = 85: T(3) = 170: T(4) = 255
70   FOR S = 1 TO 4
80   POKE 49318, T(S)
90   IF PEEK(49319) <> R(S) THEN 120
100  NEXT S
110  PRINT "TEST OF SN74";A$;" OK":END
120  PRINT "FAILURE": END
200  R(1) = 15: R(2) = 15: R(3) = 15: R(4) = 0
210  GOTO 60
300  R(1) = 0: R(2) = 0: R(3) = 0: R(4) = 15
310  GOTO 60
400  R(1) = 0: R(2) = 15: R(3) = 15: R(4) = 0
410  GOTO 60
```

The last two digits that are requested by the program are the last two digits in the device number; that is, 00 for SN7400, 08 for SN-7408, and so on. If several SN7400, SN7408 or SN7486 chips are available, you may wish to test these devices. You may wish to remove an input or an output connection to simulate a fault to check the interface and your program.

**Step 6**

It should also be possible for the computer to test logic devices such as flip-flops and counters. If you are familiar with the SN7493 4-bit binary counter, you may wish to try the following steps. If not, you may find it worthwhile to read through these steps.

The pin configuration and schematic diagram for the SN7493 counter are provided in Fig. 6-18. In order to test this device, the counter outputs must be available to the computer, and the computer must be able to reset and clock the counter chip. We will not try to test the counter exhaustively, but we will test the ability to reset the counter, and the counting function.

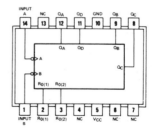

**Fig. 6-18. SN7493 4-bit counter pin configuration.**

## Step 7

Wire the SN7493 counter as shown in Fig. 6-19. You will need to use the input port and the output port from the previous steps in this experiment. You will also need two NOR gates, as shown in Fig. 6-19. A single SN7402 chip will provide these gates. Do not

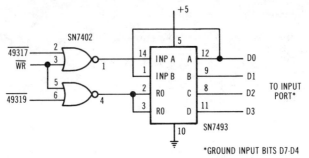

Fig. 6-19. Test circuit schematic used to check SN7493 counter chips.

substitute an SN74L93 counter for the SN7493. Remember to ground the unused inputs on the input port.

## Step 8

Write a short test program that will exercise the reset function on the counter, and one that will test the ability of the computer to clock the counter and increment its count by one.

We used the following program:

```
  10   POKE 49318,0
  20   IF PEEK(49319) > 0 THEN 1000
  30   PRINT "RESET TEST OK"
  40   FOR C = 1 TO 15
  50   POKE 49317, 0
  60   IF PEEK(49319) <> C THEN 1010
  70   NEXT C
  80   PRINT "COUNT TEST OK": END
1000   PRINT "RESET FAILURE":END
1010   PRINT "COUNT FAILURE AT "; C: END
```

The program first tests the reset and then starts the necessary tests to test the ability of the chip to increment its count by one for each pulse that is received at the INP A pin.

**Step 9**

This program does not test all 16 counter states. The last count from 1111 to 0000 is not tested. Could you change the program to take care of this?

It should not be difficult for you to add the final test to the program. There are several ways in which you could do this. Here is one:

```
 90   POKE 49317,0
100   IF PEEK(49319) <> 0 THEN 1010
110   PRINT "COUNT TEST OK": END
```

In this case, a final count has been generated and the "wrap-around" count from 1111 to 0000 has been tested.

The output port will not be used again, so you may remove it from your breadboard. The input port will be used again. The power may be turned off, since the program will not be used again.

**EXPERIMENT NO. 15**
**SIMPLE FLAG CIRCUITS**

**Purpose**

The purpose of this experiment is to demonstrate the construction and use of simple flag circuits.

**Discussion**

Flags are signals that are used by the computer and I/O devices so that their operations are synchronized. Flags are commonly used to indicate one of two possible conditions, ready/busy, full/empty, hot/cold, and other combinations that relate the conditions of an interface to the computer. Experiment No. 6 illustrated the use of input ports to transfer nonnumeric information to the computer. This experiment will develop this concept further. An 8-bit input port is required in this experiment.

## Pin Configuration of the Integrated Circuit (Fig. 6-20)

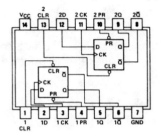

Fig. 6-20. SN7474 dual D-type flip-flop chip
pin configuration.

### Step 1

An input port will be required in this experiment. You should be able to construct an input-port circuit without further instructions. Many of the previous experiments have detailed the construction of such ports, and we recommend that you use one of these circuits. Once your input port has been wired and tested, go on to the next step.

### Step 2

One of the previous experiments investigated the use of simple switches as sensor or flag inputs. This experiment will use flip-flop circuits in place of the mechanical switches or jumper wires. Wire the circuit shown in Fig. 6-21.

A jumper wire should be used as the connection between +5 volts and the clear input, pin 1, so that you can clear the flag by moving the wire from +5 volts to ground and then back to +5 volts. The pulser circuit may be a pair of cross-coupled NAND gates, or an equivalent circuit that will generate "clean" noise-free logic transitions. This type of function is described in the appendix.

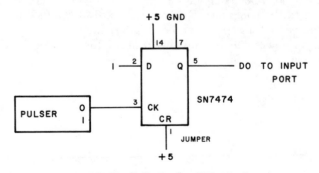

Fig. 6-21. Simple flip-flop-based flag circuit.

## Step 3

How would you program the computer so that the logic state at bit D0 of the input port could be monitored? Assume that there are two possible conditions:(a) the other bits are grounded (logic zero), or (b) the other bits may be used for other flag inputs.

If the other bits are grounded, then the value from the input port will be zero when the flag is cleared, and nonzero when it is set. If the other bits are used for flag inputs, then the "unwanted" bits must be masked. The masking operation uses the logical AND operation, so an assembly-language subroutine would have to be used.

## Step 4

In this case, you will enter the assembly-language program that is used to perform the AND operation on two data bytes. Follow these steps to enter the program:

1. Press the RESET key and type CALL -151 and press the RE-TURN key. The Apple should respond with an asterisk (°) when it is in the Monitor mode.
2. Type 0300:00 00 00 48 AD 00 03 2D 01 03 8D 02 03 68 60 Leave a space between the two-digit groups as shown. Use 00 for the first three values in the program.
3. Press the RETURN key, type 02FF and press the RETURN key three times. Now, check the data shown on the display with the information that you entered.

To test this assembly-language routine, you may use the following program. Since the AND operation will use binary numbers, you will have to convert your test numbers into binary so that you can check the results.

```
1000   POKE 10,76: POKE 11,03: POKE 12,03
1010   INPUT " MASK BYTE ";M: POKE 768,M
1020   INPUT " DATA BYTE ";D: POKE 769,D
1030   Q = USR(0): PRINT "ANSWER "; PEEK(770)
1040   GOTO 1010
```

If the program does not provide the proper results, re-enter the Monitor mode and check the data bytes that you have entered.

You should realize that the POKE commands in line 1000 are used to set up pointer address bytes so that the USR command can "locate" the assembly-language subroutine that you entered. We refer you to Chapter 4 and to Experiment No. 7 for more information about this type of assembly-language subroutine use.

## Step 5

Now that you have entered the assembly-language program that will AND two bytes to yield an 8-bit result, you will use it to test the flag bit. What would you use as the mask byte?

Since the flag is being input to the computer at bit D0, only the least-significant bit (LSB) would be "set," so the mask would be $00000001_2$, or $1_{10}$. The mask byte is placed in address 768, as you can probably tell from the test program in the previous step.

## Step 6

Write a short program that could be used to test the flip-flop flag circuit. The Apple should print a "0" if the flag is cleared, or a "1" if the flag is set. You can reset the flag manually by moving the jumper wire that connects flip-flop pin 1 and +5 volts so that pin 1 is momentarily connected to ground.

We used the following program:

```
10   POKE 10,76: POKE 11,3: POKE 12,3
20   POKE 768,1
30   POKE 769,PEEK(49319)
40   Z = USR(0)
50   IF PEEK(770) = 0 THEN 80
60   PRINT "1"
70   GOTO 30
80   PRINT "0"
90   GOTO 30
```

This program seemed to work very well. Could you "invert" the program so that a logic 0 would be sensed as the on condition, and so that a logic one would be sensed as the off condition?

Yes. Simply reverse the commands at lines 60 and 80. You can easily "invert" the sense of a flag in software.

**Step 7**

In this step, you will use a short program that will count the number of times that the flag is set. Again, the assembly-language subroutine will be used. You may wish to add another pulser circuit to provide the flag-clearing operation to replace the jumper wire between pin 1 on the SN7474 and +5 volts.

Enter the following program and run it:

```
10   POKE 10,76: POKE 11,3: POKE 12,3
20   POKE 768,1
30   HOME: C = 0
40   POKE 769, PEEK(49319)
50   Z = USR(0)
60   IF PEEK(770) = 0 THEN 40
70   C = C+1: HTAB 1: VTAB 1: PRINT C
80   GOTO 40
```

Be sure that the flip-flop is cleared before you test the program. With the program running, actuate the pulser and set the flip-flop. What do you observe? Is this what you expected?

We found that the count started as soon as the flip-flop was set, and that it continued for as long as the flag remained set. Clearing the flip-flop stopped the count. What we really wanted was one count each time the flip-flop was set.

Why didn't this happen as expected? The set state of the flip-flop continued to be tested and detected by the program. We could not reset the flip-flop fast enough by hand to stop the counting at one count per pulser actuation.

**Step 8**

In most computer systems, the computer, or the flag-containing device clears the flag after it has been detected. To allow your interface to clear the flip-flop, add the circuit shown in Fig. 6-22. You will need an SN7402 NOR-gate chip. Be sure that you wire the +5-volt power supply to pin 14, and ground to pin 7, on the SN7402 chip. Since the NOR-gate circuit will provide the reset signal for the flip-

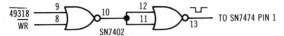

Fig. 6-22. Simple flag-clearing circuit schematic.

flop, be sure that you remove the wire that was used to connect +5 volts to pin 1 on the SN7474 flip-flop.

The circuit shown in Fig. 6-22 will allow you to clear the flip-flop with a POKE 49318 command.

Modify your program so that line 65 is added:

65  POKE 49318,0

When this command is executed, the flag will be cleared. Since you may not know the state of the flag when you start the program, you might want to add a flag-clearing command at the start of the program, too. Now run the program. When the flag is detected, the flag is immediately cleared. Then the count is incremented and displayed.

One of the benefits of using this type of flag, and using the assembly-language subroutine to check the flag, is that you do not "stall" the computer waiting for a flag, unless you want to. Thus, you can write a program to check for a flag. If the flag is not present, the computer goes about some other task. If the flag is set, the device associated with it is serviced, and the computer then goes on.

The BASIC interpreter in the Apple has a flag-checking command called WAIT. This command may be used to test for a flag, but if the flag is not found, the program continues to wait for it, and it cannot do anything else. If a program "hangs up" waiting for a flag that never occurs, you must press the RESET key to re-establish control of the Apple. We refer you to *Basic Programming Reference Manual* for the Apple for more information about the WAIT command. This command does not incorporate any flag-clearing commands.

**EXPERIMENT NO. 16**
**A SIMPLE ANALOG-TO-DIGITAL CONVERTER**

### Purpose

In this experiment, you will interface an 8-bit analog-to-digital converter to the computer. Several different types of measurements will be made.

### Discussion

There are many applications for analog-to-digital converters, or A/D converters in computer systems. The A/D converters allow the computer to measure analog voltages such as those that would arise from various signal sources and transducers. In this experiment, a simple 8-bit A/D converter will be used. The converter is a National Semiconductor ADC0804-type converter. This converter has three-state outputs, so it can be interfaced directly to a microcomputer data bus without difficulty. However, the three-state outputs have an access time that can be as long as 200 nanoseconds. Thus, if you attempt to use the ADC0804 A/D converter on your interface bread-board, you will find that the additional time required to actuate the bus interlocking circuitry to turn the data bus around for input will be too long. The data from the converter will be "missed" by the computer.

In order to perform this experiment, you must have access to the "bare" Apple data bus. This is explained in the following steps.

## Pin Configuration of the Integrated Circuit (Fig. 6-23)

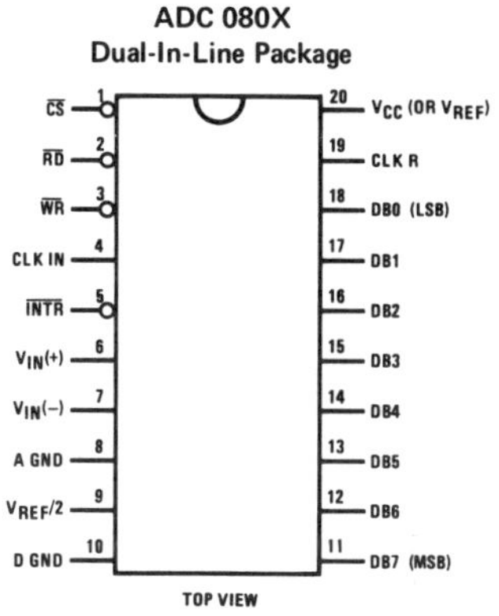

Fig. 6-23. Pin configuration of the ADC0804 A/D converter.

**ADC 080X**
**Dual-In-Line Package**

| Pin | Signal | Pin | Signal |
|---|---|---|---|
| 1 | $\overline{CS}$ | 20 | $V_{CC}$ (OR $V_{REF}$) |
| 2 | $\overline{RD}$ | 19 | CLK R |
| 3 | $\overline{WR}$ | 18 | DB0 (LSB) |
| 4 | CLK IN | 17 | DB1 |
| 5 | $\overline{INTR}$ | 16 | DB2 |
| 6 | $V_{IN}(+)$ | 15 | DB3 |
| 7 | $V_{IN}(-)$ | 14 | DB4 |
| 8 | A GND | 13 | DB5 |
| 9 | $V_{REF}/2$ | 12 | DB6 |
| 10 | D GND | 11 | DB7 (MSB) |

TOP VIEW

## Step 1

In this experiment, you will interface the ADC0804 A/D converter directly to the data bus as it comes from the Apple. To do this, carefully remove the two 8216 bus buffer chips at IC-10 and IC-11 on your interface breadboard.

## Step 2

Wire the ADC0804 integrated circuit as shown in Fig. 6-24. The data bus lines are placed into the corresponding holes at the sockets for IC-10 and IC-11. If the wires do not fit into the holes very easily, we suggest placing a 16-pin socket with larger access holes in the sockets at IC-10 and IC-11. This will allow you to make the connections without having to force the wires in the small holes. The wires should fit into the corresponding holes without much force. If excessive force is used, you may bend the socket contacts so that they

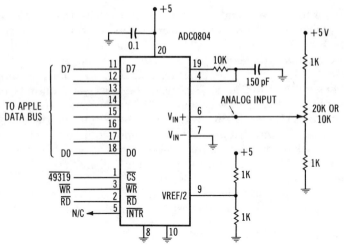

Fig. 6-24. ADC0804 interface circuit schematic.

do not make proper contact with the 8216 chips when they are re-inserted into their respective sockets.

## Step 3

Enter the following program into your computer and run it:

```
10  POKE 49319,0
20  FOR T = 0 TO 100: NEXT T
30  PRINT PEEK(49319)
40  GOTO 10
```

What does the program do? What is displayed on the video screen?

The program exercises the A/D converter, starting a conversion, providing a time delay so that the conversion can be performed, and then reading and displaying the data. Slowly adjust the potentiometer as you observe the data to confirm that the converter is operating.

As you change the voltage setting of the potentiometer, you should see a corresponding change in the value displayed by the Apple. What is the minimum value? What is the maximum value? Does this seem to be what you would expect?

The minimum value should be in the range of 0 or 1. The maximum value should be between 253 and 255. This is what is expected from an 8-bit device, since it can only generate values between 0 and 255.

**Step 4**

The ADC0804 chip has a flag output that can be used to monitor the status of the converter; that is, busy or ready. This output is a logic zero when data is ready for the computer, and it is a logic one when the converter is performing a conversion. This output is really the output of a flag circuit, and the flag is reset when the eight data bits are read into the computer. Since the converter can perform many thousands of conversions in a second, is there any need to monitor this flag signal?

Probably not, since the converter will complete the conversion process before the data can be accessed by a BASIC-language program. Can you suggest some possible uses for the flag output?

The flag could be used for assembly-language A/D converter programming. In assembly-language programs, the flag could be tested as an input to an input port, or it could be used with the interrupt on the 6502 microprocessor chip. Since these are high-speed applications, it would be useful to monitor the flag to determine when the converter had finished a conversion.

**Step 5**

Remove line 20 from your program and run the program. What do you find?

The data values are the same as those observed when the program was used with the time delay steps. Thus, the converter is "outrunning" the BASIC control program.

**Step 6**

The values displayed on the screen do not represent the actual voltage that is being measured, but are an 8-bit binary representation. Write a program that will perform the conversion to voltages. You may add the steps to the program already in use.

We used the following steps which simply perform a mathematical conversion of the decimal value 0 to 255 to a corresponding voltage 0 to +5 volts.

```
10  POKE 49319,0
20  FOR T = 0 TO 100: NEXT T
30  PRINT (PEEK(49319)*5/255)
40  GOTO 10
```

Try our program, or your own. Does it work?

It should. You will see that the computer prints many decimal digits, probably too many, since the converter is only accurate to a maximum of one part in 256, or about 0.25%. Unfortunately, rounding is not a trivial task in the Apple. You can perform either a mathematical rounding, or you can use a string operation to print only a selected number of digits after the decimal point. You can use the following if you wish:

```
30  A$ = STR$(PEEK(49319)*5/255)
40  PRINT LEFT$ (A$,4)
50  GOTO 10
```

Remember that this routine simply *limits* the displayed value to four decimal digits. It does not perform any rounding.

### Step 7

Try to write a routine that will use the high-resolution graphics capability of the Apple computer, so that the program will plot the voltage values with respect to time. The measurements should be taken at a regular time (time-delay program), and a continuous line-plot should be drawn. If you are not familiar with the high-resolution graphics formats and commands, use the program provided below:

```
100  HRG: HCOLOR = 3: Y1 =0
110  FOR X = 0 TO 249
120  POKE 49319,0
```

```
130   Y2  =  PEEK(49319)/1.594
140   HPLOT X,Y1 TO X+1, Y2
150   Y1  =  Y2
160   NEXT X
170   END
```

Try this program. Vary the potentiometer setting as the program is running. The plot should appear as the changes are made. A constant voltage will give you a horizontal line on the screen.

## Step 8

Can you suggest a simple experiment that would demonstrate the use of the A/D converter and the graphics program?

There are several simple experiments that you might like to try. Each involves measuring a voltage that is proportional to the physical measurement that is being made. For example, you could measure the voltage across a photocell in changing light conditions, a voltage across a charging capacitor, or a voltage that is proportional to temperature.

Wire the circuit shown in Fig. 6-25. In this circuit, you will use the A/D converter and computer to measure a charging voltage across a large electrolytic capacitor.

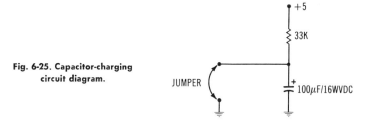

Fig. 6-25. Capacitor-charging circuit diagram.

Use the jumper wire to discharge the capacitor, and leave it in place until after you have started the program. Once the program is running, remove the jumper to ground. You should see the voltage slowly increase, as the capacitor is charged. Why does the graph show the zero-voltage point on the top of the screen, and the high-voltage point on the bottom?

The computer plots from the top to the bottom in increasing values, so if you want to invert the display, you will have to "invert" the values from the converter. This means that you will need to convert a zero into 159, and a 159 into a zero. To do this, simply change line 130 to:

```
130   Y2  =  160 − (PEEK(49319)/1.594)
```

## Step 9

You can also use the A/D converter to measure temperature. An LM335 temperature sensor may be used to generate a voltage that is proportional to temperature, at a rate of 10 mV/K. The Kelvin scale of temperature uses the same units of degrees as the Celsius scale, except that 0°C = 273K. Thus, a room temperature of 20°C will be the equivalent of 293K, and the LM335 will generate 293 × 10 mV as its output, or 2.93 volts.

To measure temperature, wire the circuit shown in Fig. 6-26. Be sure that the potentiometer or capacitor-charging circuit is not connected to the A/D converter input at the same time as the temperature sensor.

You can use the same graphical display program that was used in the previous step, but you may wish to add a time-delay step at line 155:

```
155   FOR T  =  0 TO 100: NEXT T
```

This will delay the display, since the temperature changes will be slower than the capacitor-charging voltage changes.

Run the program. Heat the sensor with your fingers. Do you observe any change? What do you expect to see?

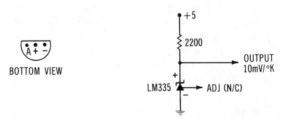

Fig. 6-26. Schematic for a temperature-measuring circuit, and pin configuration for LM335 chip.

You probably will not see much change, since the display is set up for a range of 0 to 500K, as represented by 0 volts to +5 volts from the sensor. If you see more than a few "points" increase in the display, you have significantly warmed the sensor. You can more readily cool the sensor with some moisture, or with a can of freeze-spray that is used to cool electronic components. If this is not available, a piece of ice can be used to cool the sensor.

Could you "expand" the display to provide a more useful display of the temperature changes? How could you do this?

There are several ways of "expanding" the display. If you know that the temperatures will only vary between 200 and 300K, you could change the software so that the display on the screen represented voltages between +2 and +3 volts. However, keep in mind that you have not increased the resolution of the converter in doing this. There will still be the same number of discrete voltage steps in the converter's range. You have only expanded the display of these values.

You could also use some other circuits. Operational amplifiers could be used to scale the voltage range of +2 to +3 volts to 0–5 volts, so that the entire temperature range of 200 to 300K would generate 0–5 volts. This could be measured by the converter and displayed on the screen. Now, the resolution has been increased, since the entire 256 different voltages are used in the temperature range of interest.

There is much more to analog-converter interfacing, but we hope that this experiment has interested you in the use of these important devices. For additional interfacing ideas and techniques, we refer you to *TRS-80 Interfacing, Book 2,* and *Microcomputer-Analog Converter Software and Hardware Interfacing* ( Howard W. Sams & Co., Inc., Indianapolis, IN 46268 ).

Please note that in this experiment, we generated a reference voltage of +2.5 volts by using two 1000-ohm resistors to divide the +5-volt supply in half. In precision analog-converter applications, a +2.500-volt reference is used in place of the resistors. We have chosen to use the resistors in this experiment because they are inexpensive and easy to set up. However, they produce results that are not as accurate as would be needed for precision measurements. There are many reference devices and circuits available, as noted in the references mentioned above.

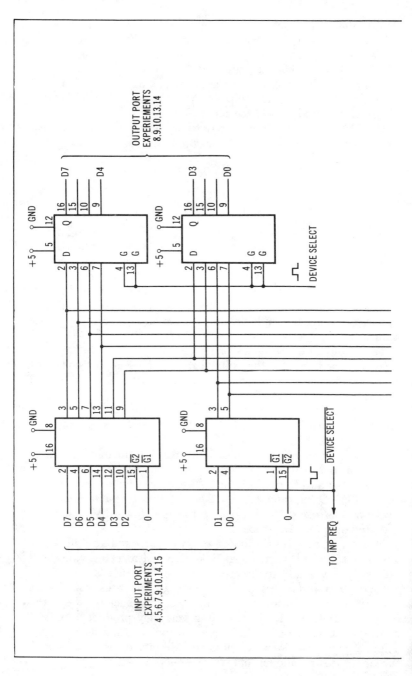

Fig. 6-27. Generalized I/O ports and control

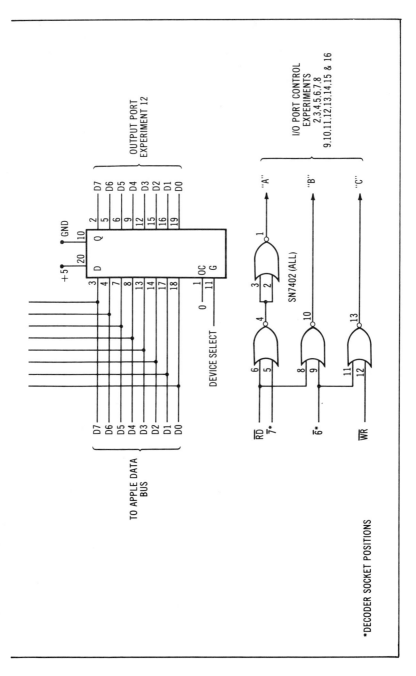

circuit schematic for the experiments.

# CHAPTER 7

# On the Bus

While many readers will be content to perform some of the experiments in the previous chapter, and go no further with the design and development of interfaces, there are others who will be interested in developing special-purpose interface circuits that will become a permanent part of their computer system. This chapter is written for this reader. We will describe how you can design special interface circuits that can take advantage of many of the built-in features of the Apple computer.

If you want to construct an interface circuit that will be used again and again, you will want to construct it on something other than a solderless breadboard. Breadboarded circuits take up workspace, they are messy and frequently come apart at the worst possible moment. The alternative is to construct the interface circuit in some permanent form, so that it can be mounted out of harm's way, inside the Apple case.

When the Apple computer was designed, it must have been obvious to the engineers that people would be interested in expanding the system so that various standard peripherals and nonstandard circuits could be added to the computer. Thus, they provided eight female edge connectors at the rear of the main printed circuit board, so that the important computer signals would be readily available for anyone who wanted to use them. You have already used some of these signals, since the interface that was described previously plugs into one of the available "slots."

The slots are numbered 0-7, and you can use all but slot 0, which has been reserved by the manufacturer for special expansions of the computer. Slots 1-7 are available for you to use as you wish. There

## Table 7-1. Apple Bus Signals and Descriptions

| Pin | Name | Description |
|---|---|---|
| 1 | I/O SELECT | A logic zero signal, active at slot n, when the computer addresses locations CnOOH-CnFFH. Active during Φ0. Not available at slot 0. (10)* |
| 2-17 | A15-A0 | Buffered address bus lines. (5) |
| 18 | R/W | Buffered read/write control signal. (2) |
| 19 | SYNC | Video timing synchronization signal. Available only at slot 7. (?) |
| 20 | I/O STROBE | A logic zero signal, active at all slots when the computer addresses locations C8OOH-CFFFH. Active during Φo. (4) |
| 21 | RDY | Ready control input to 6502 processor. |
| 22 | DMA | Direct-memory access control input. |
| 23 | INT OUT | Interrupt daisy chain signal to adjacent slot. |
| 24 | DMA OUT | DMA daisy chain signal to adjacent slot. |
| 25 | +5 volts | +5-volt power supply connection. 500 mA maximum available to all cards. |
| 26 | GND | System electrical ground. |
| 27 | DMA IN | DMA daisy chain signal to adjacent slot. |
| 28 | INT IN | Interrupt daisy chain signal to adjacent slot. |
| 29 | NMI | Nonmaskable interrupt input to 6502 chip. Vectors processor to subroutine in 03FBH. |
| 30 | IRQ | Maskable interrupt input to 6502 chip. Address of interrupt subroutine in 03FE and 03FF. |
| 31 | RES | Input/output line. When pulled low, the Apple is reset. Interface may monitor or generate a reset. |
| 32 | INH | When pulled to a logic zero, all internal ROMs are disabled. |
| 33 | −12 V | −12-volt power supply connection. Total of 200 mA available to **all** cards. |
| 34 | −5 V | −5-volt power supply connection. Total of 200 mA available to all cards. |
| 35 | COLOR REF | This 3.580 MHz color reference signal is only present at slot 7. (?) |
| 36 | 7M | A standard 7.159 MHz reference signal. (2) |
| 37 | Q3 | A standard 2.046 MHz reference signal. (2) |
| 38 | Φ1 | Standard 1.023 MHz microprocessor clock signal. (2) |
| 39 | USER 1 | Logic zero input. When pulled low, all internal I/0 devices are disabled. |
| 40 | φ0 | Standard 1.023 MHz microprocessor clock signal. Complement of Φ1. (2) |
| 41 | DEVICE SELECT | Logic zero signal, one per slot. Active for 16 addresses per slot (see Table 7-3). (10) |
| 42-49 | D7-D0 | Buffered data bus signals. (1) |
| 50 | +12 V | +12-volt power supply connection. Total of 250 mA available to all cards. |

*Number in parentheses indicates the number of SN74LS00-family inputs that each signal can drive per interface slot.

are many companies that sell plug-compatible interfaces, and you can plug these into these slots without further ado.

In Chapter 5, some of the common interface signals were de-

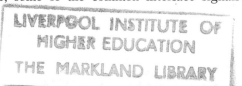

scribed; the address bus signals, the data bus signals, and some of the control signals. There are other useful signals provided at the seven available interface edge connectors. The signals are listed and described in Table 7-1.

Since you are already familiar with the data bus and address bus signals, they will not be discussed any further. Some of the other signals are important, too, and they can be used to greatly simplify the construction of interface circuits.

## INTERFACE CONTROL SIGNALS

### I/O SELECT

The I/O SELECT signal (pin 1) is active when it is a logic zero, as indicated by the "bar" above the same of the signal. Each of the seven available interface slots, 1-7, has its own $\overline{\text{I/O SELECT}}$ signal, thus this signal may be used to select a specific card. The $\overline{\text{I/O SE-}}$ $\overline{\text{LECT}}$ signal for a card slot, $n$, is active when the address bus lines are set at addresses $Cn00$ through $CnFF$, inclusive. For example, if the Apple addresses location C5AB, the $\overline{\text{I/O SELECT}}$ signal at slot 5 will be a logic zero. None of the $\overline{\text{I/O SELECT}}$ signals at the other slots will be active at this time. There will also be times when *none* of these signals is active. The range of addresses that affect the $\overline{\text{I/O}}$ $\overline{\text{SELECT}}$ signals is shown in Table 7-2.

Table 7-2. I/O SELECT Address Allocations

| Interface Slot | Address Range | |
|:---:|:---:|:---:|
| 1 | C100–C1FF | 49408–49663 |
| 2 | C200–C2FF | 49664–49919 |
| 3 | C300–C3FF | 49920–50175 |
| 4 | C400–C4FF | 50176–50431 |
| 5 | C500–C5FF | 50432–50687 |
| 6 | C600–C6FF | 50688–50943 |
| 7 | C700–C7FF | 50944–51199 |

There are a number of possible uses for this signal. Since it is active when the Apple addresses a contiguous block of 256 addresses, or one page, the signal could be used to enable a memory chip with 256 addresses. It could also be used to enable a device address decoder that could address 256 I/O devices. These applications are shown in block diagram form in Figs. 7-1 and 7-2.

You might be wondering why anyone would want to add a block of 256 bytes of memory to an Apple computer system, when the Apple can easily contain 48K of memory by itself. In some applications, it is necessary to have short assembly-language routines that can "drive" an interface. The assembly-language programs do their

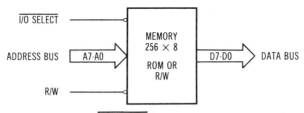

Fig. 7-1. Using I/O SELECT to control a page of memory.

job very efficiently. Such "driver routines" can be placed in read-only memory (ROM), and the ROM chip may be used in the interface circuit. In this way, the driver routines are a part of the overall interface, and they are "loaded" when the interface card is plugged in. They do not have to be loaded from cassette or disk, and they do not take any of the other memory space.

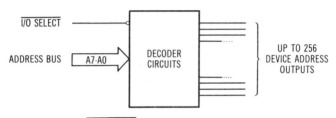

Fig. 7-2. Using I/O SELECT to control a memory address decoder.

Sometimes an interface will require a small amount of read/write (R/W) memory for temporary storage. You can also use the I/O SELECT line to control a 256 byte block of R/W memory.

Remember that each interface slot has its own I/O SELECT signal, and each signal is active when the Apple addresses a specific "page" of memory.

## I/O STROBE

The I/O STROBE signal is a logic zero signal that is provided at all of the interface slots. It is common to all of the connectors, and is not specific to any one. This signal will be a logic zero whenever the Apple accesses a location within the range C800H to CFFFH, inclusive. Thus, every card will be signalled when the address on the address bus is within this range, which covers 2048 addresses, or 2K of memory.

You may use this signal to enable memory chips and I/O devices, but you will probably want to further "qualify" this signal by gating it with some of the address bus lines, A10-A0. A simple block diagram of how this signal could be used is shown in Fig. 7-3. In this

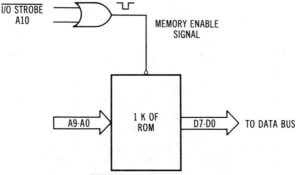

Fig. 7-3. Using I/O STROBE for 1K memory block control.

circuit, the I/O STROBE signal has been used to select a 1K block of ROM on an interface card. The remaining 1024 addresses could be divided among the other interfaces as you wish. We urge that you use caution in using this signal, however, since you may find that some manufacturers have used this line to decode memory and I/O device addresses in just this manner. Thus, you may find that you have a conflict in addressing between a commercial interface that you wish to add to your system, and one that you have already designed, built, and installed.

## DEVICE SELECT

This signal is specific to each interface slot, and it has a range of only 16 addresses for each slot, as shown in Table 7-3. The DEVICE SELECT signal is active in the logic zero state. Since the DEVICE SELECT signal is active for only a 16-address block, its use will be fairly well limited to I/O device addressing, as shown in Fig. 7-4. In this circuit, the DEVICE SELECT signal has been used to enable a 4-to-16-line decoder. If a particular interface has only a single function, and only requires a single enable signal, you may decide to use the DEVICE SELECT signal by itself, without any further decoding. This is permissible, as long as you realize that the device selected in this way will be active at 16 different addresses, C0n0H to C0nFH,

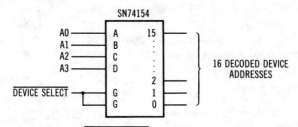

Fig. 7-4. Using DEVICE SELECT to enable a 16-address decoder.

**Table 7-3. DEVICE SELECT Address Allocations**

| Interface Slot | Address Range | |
|:---:|:---:|:---:|
| 0 | C080–C08F | 49280–49295 |
| 1 | C090–C09F | 49296–49311 |
| 2 | C0A0–C0AF | 49312–49327 |
| 3 | C0B0–C0BF | 49328–49343 |
| 4 | C0C0–C0CF | 49344–49359 |
| 5 | C0D0–C0DF | 49360–49375 |
| 6 | C0E0–C0EF | 49376–49391 |
| 7 | C0F0–C0FF | 49392–49407 |

inclusive. This use of the signal also limits your ability to add other functions to the interface, should you decide to expand it at a later time.

## $\overline{IRQ}$ and $\overline{NMI}$

These are the two interrupt inputs to the 6502 microprocessor chip. The $\overline{IRQ}$ (interrupt request) is maskable, and it can be disabled by using the appropriate software steps. The $\overline{NMI}$ (nonmaskable interrupt) is always active.

These interrupt input lines are common to all of the seven interface slots, with the $\overline{IRQ}$ signal connected at pin 30, and the $\overline{NMI}$ signal connected at pin 29. In most interface circuits, the $\overline{NMI}$ line would be dedicated to one peripheral, and that must be recognized, no matter what. The $\overline{IRQ}$ line would be shared among many interface circuits. Appropriate software steps would be required within the interrupt service subroutine so that the computer could detect which device had actually requested the interrupt. Each of the interrupting devices could have a 1-bit input port that could be read to determine the status of its interrupt flag. A typical interrupt flag circuit is shown in Fig. 7-5. Notice that the flag is cleared under software control.

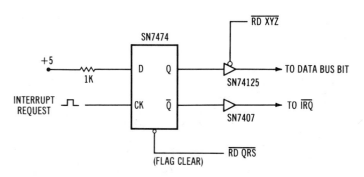

Fig. 7-5. Interrupt flag circuit diagram.

If this type of a "polled" interrupt is used, with the computer polling each of the devices that could have generated an interrupt, a priority can be established in the software. Thus, if the computer checks the devices in the order A, B, C, and so on, device A has the highest priority, since it will be checked first when an interrupt is detected.

The interface slots also have two other interrupt lines that may be of interest, depending upon your application. These signals are the interrupt input (INT IN) at pin 28, and the interrupt output (INT OUT) at pin 23. These signals are used to "daisy chain" interrupt signals form one card to the next. The signals are only connected between the interface connectors, as shown in Fig. 7-6. Thus, the INT OUT signal on slot 1 is connected to the INT IN signal on slot 2, the INT OUT on slot 2 is connected to the INT IN on slot 3, and so on. The INT IN and IN OUT lines are only connected to the adjacent interface slot, and they do not go any further.

REAR OF APPLE

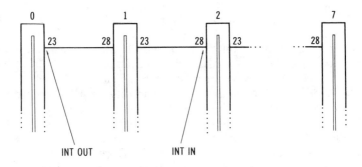

*NOTATIONS ARE INTERCHANGEABLE, DEPENDING UPON USE.

**Fig. 7-6. INT IN and INT OUT bus signals.**

A simple daisy-chained interrupt scheme is shown in Fig. 7-7. The lower-priority interrupting devices are further down the chain, further from the $\overline{\text{INT}}$ connection to the 6502 microprocessor chip. In this circuit, a higher priority device can pass its interrupt request up the chain, blocking any interrupt requests from the lower priority devices that are further down the chain. Once the higher-priority device has been serviced and its interrupt flag has been cleared, it will "open" its gate and allow the lower priority interrupt request to pass on to the computer.

As you can see, the computer still needs some way of determining which device is generating the interrupt, so that it can select the corresponding interrupt service subroutine. This type of interrupt

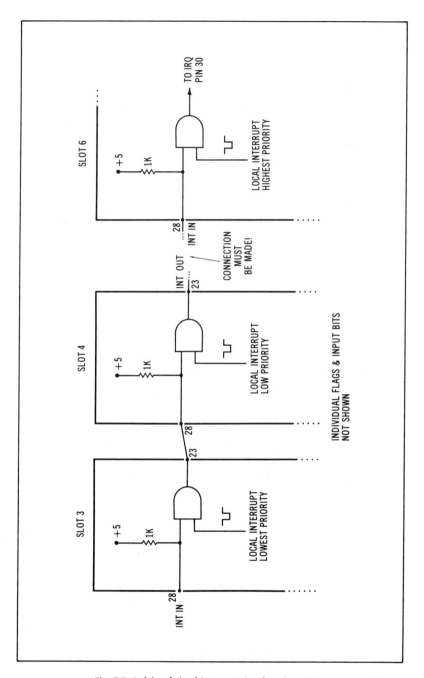

Fig. 7-7. A daisy-chained interrupt signal configuration.

scheme is quite complex, and we recommend using the simple interrupt flag circuit provided in Fig. 7-5. This should be sufficient for most uses. In the daisy-chain configuration, you cannot have "empty," or open, slots between interface circuit boards, since this will break the INT IN/INT OUT circuit "chain." Enough said about interrupts. For more information, we refer you to *Programming & Interfacing the 6502, With Experiments* (Howard W. Sams & Co., Inc., Indianapolis, IN 46268).

## $\overline{\text{DMA}}$

The $\overline{\text{DMA}}$ input is used to allow an external device to address memory locations without first having to go through the 6502 microprocessor. Thus, *the external device has direct memory access*, or DMA. Since several devices could request a direct memory access transfer of information, a daisy-chained set of peripherals is possible, since the interface slots have DMA IN and DMA OUT pins that connect to the adjacent interface connectors. Direct memory access interfaces are not trivial design projects, and we recommend that you thoroughly understand the operation of the 6502 microprocessor chip and its associated circuitry before you attempt to use this feature.

## $\overline{\text{RES}}$

The reset line at pin 31, $\overline{\text{RES}}$, is actually a bidirectional signal line. You can use this line to reset your interface circuits, since it will be a logic zero when the Apple is reset when power is applied, or when the RESET pushbutton is pressed. You can also force the Apple into a reset condition by grounding this line. If you choose to use this line to reset the Apple from your interface, a high-current open-collector gate or buffer must be used to pull the line to ground. An SN7407 open-collector buffer chip could be used in this type of circuit. The $\overline{\text{RES}}$ signal line is common to all of the interface slots.

## $\overline{\text{INH}}$

In the Apple computer, you can substitute your own assembly-language programs for the programs stored in the BASIC interpreter ROMs. By pulling the $\overline{\text{INH}}$ line at pin 32 to ground, you will inhibit *all* of the BASIC interpreter and Monitor ROMs, so that your own programs can control the entire system. Since there is some room already available for this type of operation, you probably won't use this function, since you would not have access to any of the useful subroutines within the standard ROMs supplied with the Apple. It would be difficult, for example, to control the display, without the subroutines in the BASIC interpreter ROMs. You will need an open-collector buffer chip to pull this line to ground, if you choose to use this function.

## USER 1

This input will allow you to inhibit the generation of all of the $\overline{\text{I/O SELECT}}$ and $\overline{\text{DEVICE SELECT}}$ signals within the Apple computer, so that you can "turn off" all of the I/O devices. This line must be pulled down to a logic zero to cause this action. To prevent the accidental use of this line, you must use a wire jumper to connect two solder pads on the main printed circuit board of the Apple, before the USER 1 signal can be used. We refer you to the *Apple II Reference Manual* for the necessary details.

Since your primary purpose in using the $\overline{\text{I/O SELECT}}$ and $\overline{\text{DE-VICE SELECT}}$ signals is to simplify your interface design, there is probably no need to use this line, unless you wish to do some sort of expansion of the computer system with I/O devices that are external to the basic system, or that might use some of the memory addresses that have been assigned to the $\overline{\text{I/O SELECT}}$ and $\overline{\text{DEVICE SELECT}}$ signals. The USER 1 signal is present at pin 39 on the interface connectors.

## RDY

There are times when it is necessary to slightly "delay" the 6502 microprocessor so that an external I/O device, or memory chip will have sufficient time to access its data and present it on the data bus. The ready input ( RDY ) found at pin 21 on each of the interface connectors can be used to put the 6502 in a "wait" condition when it is grounded. This input must be synchronized with the microprocessor clock, and it should change its state during the $\Phi_1$ clock logic one state. The RDY input was used in older 6502-based computers, since older memory devices could not access their data as fast as required by the computer. Thus, when they were addresses, they had to put the 6502 into a "wait" condition for several clock cycles until their data was available. We doubt that you will find much use for this signal, except in specialized interfaces.

## Clock Signals

There are six clock signals that are available for interface use. These are $\Phi_0$, $\Phi_1$, Q3, 7M, COLOR REF, and SYNC. The $\Phi_0$ and $\Phi_1$ are the main timing clock signals, running at 1 MHz. The clock signals are the inverse of one another. These signals are used to co-ordinate external I/O operations with the normal flow of data on the bus. As shown in Fig. 5-12, the $\Phi_1$ signal is used to control the generation of the $\overline{\text{RD}}$ and $\overline{\text{WR}}$ signals for external I/O devices. *The $\overline{\text{I/O}}$ $\overline{\text{SELECT}}$ and $\overline{\text{DEVICE SELECT}}$ signals at the I/O connectors have already been gated, or "qualified," with the $\phi_1$ clock signal.*

The Q3 signal is a 2 MHz clock signal that is asymmetric; that is,

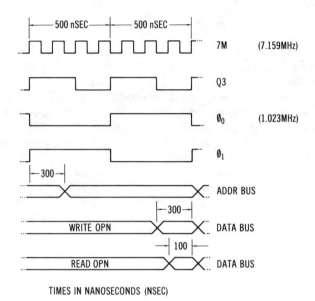

**Fig. 7-8. Timing diagram for various Apple clock signals.**

it is not a square wave. The 7M signal is a 7 MHz clock signal that is a square wave. The clock signals are derived from the main clock circuitry within the Apple, and their timing relationships are shown in Fig. 7-8. We refer you to a complete data sheet for the 6502 microprocessor for additional information about the 6502 timing relationships.

The COLOR REF and SYNC signals are available only at interface slot 7. The COLOR REF signal is the 3.5 MHz color reference signal generated by the video clock circuit in the Apple. The SYNC signal is the video timing synchronization signal. You will probably not use these signals in your interface designs unless you will be using video control circuits.

### Power

The interface connectors provide access to four standard voltages and to ground. The voltages provided are +12, −12, +5, and −5 volts. The current for each of these voltages is limited to a few hundred milliamperes, so you should consider the use of low-power interface chips, such as those found in the SN74LS00 family.

### Other Considerations

The bus-driving capability of the interface signals is quite limited, with most signals limited to driving only a few SN74LS00-type inputs. You must be careful in your design that you do not overload these signals by expecting them to drive more chip inputs than they can. If you need additional power from these signals so that they can drive more inputs on an interface card, you must buffer the signals with appropriate buffer chips. Just keep in mind that the buffers will need some additional power from the power supplies, and there is not a great deal of "extra" power at the interface connectors. Thus, you must balance your needs for signal buffering with the available power. You could always use an external power supply to power some of the interface cards, but this defeats the purpose behind putting the interface circuits in the Apple enclosure in the first place.

## AN INTERFACING EXAMPLE

Now that most of the useful interface signals have been described, let's take a close look at a typical interface circuit that can be used with the Apple computer. In many applications, it is necessary for the computer to communicate with other devices. These may include printers, controllers, remote data acquisition stations, and maybe even other computers. In most cases, a form of serial communication is used, so that long lengths of multiconductor cables are not required. Most serial communication schemes use three or four wires, so that the information that is to be exchanged is transmitted in serial fashion, bit by bit, over the wire. One set of wires is used for transmitting, and the other set is used for receiving. Such communication is usually called asynchronous-serial communication, since there is no common clock signal, or reference, that connects the two systems.

Most of the microprocessor chip manufacturers have developed some type of communication chip for their family of microprocessors. In fact, you can even "cross" families, so that a communication chip that was developed for the 8080A family can be used with a 6502 processor. In fact, that is exactly what we plan to do in this example; an 8251 universal synchronous/asynchronous receiver-transmitter chip will be interfaced to the Apple computer, right at the interface slot. We will not provide you with a great deal of detail about the operation of the USART chip, since this has been covered in detail in *TRS-80 Interfacing, Book 2* (Howard W. Sams & Co., Inc., Indianapolis, IN 46268). A magazine article covering the subject is also available. See "Cross-Pollinating the Apple," *Byte*, April, 1979, p. 24.

Since the 8251 USART chip is a bus-compatible chip, it should not be too difficult to interface the Apple. A pin configuration and block diagram for the USART are provided in Fig. 7-9. You should be able to recognize the data bus inputs, the $\overline{RD}$ and $\overline{WR}$ control inputs and a chip select input, $\overline{CS}$. Since the USART contains two sets of registers, there must be some way of distinguishing between them. The

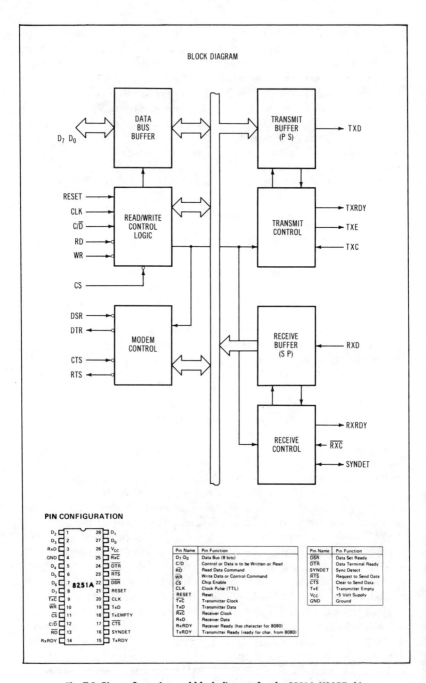

BLOCK DIAGRAM

PIN CONFIGURATION

| Pin Name | Pin Function |
|---|---|
| $D_7$-$D_0$ | Data Bus (8 bits) |
| C/D | Control or Data is to be Written or Read |
| RD | Read Data Command |
| WR | Write Data or Control Command |
| CS | Chip Enable |
| CLK | Clock Pulse (TTL) |
| RESET | Reset |
| TxC | Transmitter Clock |
| TxD | Transmitter Data |
| RxC | Receiver Clock |
| RxD | Receiver Data |
| RxRDY | Receiver Ready (has character for 8080) |
| TxRDY | Transmitter Ready (ready for char. from 8080) |

| Pin Name | Pin Function |
|---|---|
| DSR | Data Set Ready |
| DTR | Data Terminal Ready |
| SYNDET | Sync Detect |
| RTS | Request to Send Data |
| CTS | Clear to Send Data |
| TxE | Transmitter Empty |
| $V_{CC}$ | +5 Volt Supply |
| GND | Ground |

**Fig. 7-9. Pin configuration and block diagram for the 8251A USART chip.**

CONTROL/$\overline{\text{DATA}}$ input at pin 12 (C/$\overline{\text{D}}$) performs this function. A logic one selects the control mode, or command mode, while a logic zero selects the data mode. One of the address bits can be connected to this input to allow the computer to access each of the internal registers by using one address for the command register and another address for the data register.

Since the USART will be communicating with other asynchronous-serial devices, there are standard data rates that must be used to assure that the data rates of the transmitting instrument and the receiving computer are fairly close. A Motorola MC14411 bit rate generator chip has been chosen to perform this function, since it is crystal controlled. There are other popular clock-generating schemes, too.

Since the standard logic levels provided by SN7400 family transistor-transistor logic (TTL) devices cannot be used to drive long communication lines, you will need to choose whether you wish to use 20 mA current-loop signals or standard RS-232C control levels. The necessary level-conversion circuits are easy to obtain, and they are detailed in the references noted previously.

Since any sort of communication interface is useless without the software to drive it, you will need some software routines that can drive the USART chip. For the most part, these will be simple, and you may wish to use BASIC-language programs for control purposes. If you choose to use assembly-language programming, you might consider putting your control programs in ROM, and putting the ROM right on the interface board. Since there are 256 bytes of address space available for each interface slot, a small ROM can be accommodated. The 256-byte space is quite enough for some USART control programs. You can use the Monitor to test your assembly-language programs before they are put into ROM.

A complete USART interface is shown in Fig. 7-10. *This circuit has been wired and tested in our Apple computer.* If you wish to use this circuit in your computer, we suggest that you obtain the data sheets for the 8251 or 8251A USART chip, and the Motorola MC-14411 bit-rate generator chip, so that you will understand how they work. In Fig. 7-11, we have provided a general addressing circuit for a 256-byte block of ROM, which could be used to store the assembly-language USART control routines. The actual circuit would depend upon the particular ROM chip, or chips that you choose to use. In this circuit, Fairchild 93427 ROMs have been used. These are fast, bipolar, fusible-link ROMs. Each chip contains 1024 bits, organized in 256 4-bit words, so two chips are required for a complete 8-bit word. Slow, erasable PROM chips are not recommended, since their access times are fairly slow, and they could cause problems. Most of these devices contain many more locations than you can use.

You can build this circuit on a standard interface wire-wrap card, or on another type of suitable prototype card that can be plugged into one of the available interface slots. If you use the wire-wrap prototype technique, you will find that the wire-wrap pins and the chips stick out from both sides of the card, making it difficult to use the adjacent interface slots.

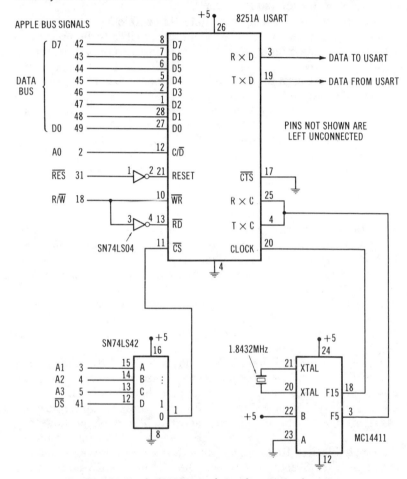

Fig. 7-10. Simple USART-to-Apple interface circuit schematic.

In our computer system, we used the USART interface in slot 3, so that the USART was addressed as devices 49328 and 49329. The registers at address 49328 are the receiver and transmitter registers, while the registers at address 49329 are the control and flag registers. Keep in mind that you can have two registers for each address, since one is a write-to register, and the other is a read-from register. If you

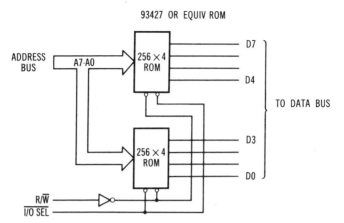

Fig. 7-11. A 256-byte memory expansion circuit diagram.

moved the card to another interface slot, the addresses for the USART would change, as noted in Table 7-3.

To use the USART interface, you must first initialize the chip with some control information that is sent as two consecutive bytes to the control register. Don't worry about sending two bytes to the same register, the USART "knows" what to do with them. After the USART has been initialized, you can use it to transmit and receive asynchronous-serial streams of information. The program shown in Example 7-1 can be used to transmit an 8-bit byte of data, while the program shown in Example 7-2 can be used to receive an 8-bit byte.

#### Example 7-1. USART Transmitter Control Subroutine

```
1010   POKE 49320, TX
1020   WAIT 49329, 1
1030   RETURN
```

#### Example 7-2. USART Receiver Control Subroutine

```
1050   WAIT 49329, 2
1060   RX = PEEK(49328)
1070   RETURN
```

The software checks the necessary flags so that the transmitter transmits its data only when it is ready, and the receiver only provides data when it has actually received some.

The main point here has been to develop a simple interface that uses many of the Apple bus interface control signals, so that you can see how they work. It is also nice to know that the interface example actually works, and that it can be used in some real applications. We hope that you have seen how easy it is to develop an interface for the Apple, based upon the concepts of port addressing, port control, and flags, that we introduced throughout the book.

APPENDIX **A**

# Logic Functions

In the experiments in this book, several logic functions are required. These functions are noted as lamp monitors, logic switches, and pulsers. In each case, the equivalent circuits are simple, but rather than duplicate them in each schematic diagram, block diagrams have been used. The following sections describe each of the functions that are required.

## LAMP MONITORS

Lamp monitors are simply light-emitting diodes, or other on-off indicating devices that are used to indicate the state of a logical output. We have adopted the convention of logic one being the lit, or on state, and logic zero being the unlit, or off, state. The two circuits shown in Fig. A-1 may be used to construct lamp monitors. The

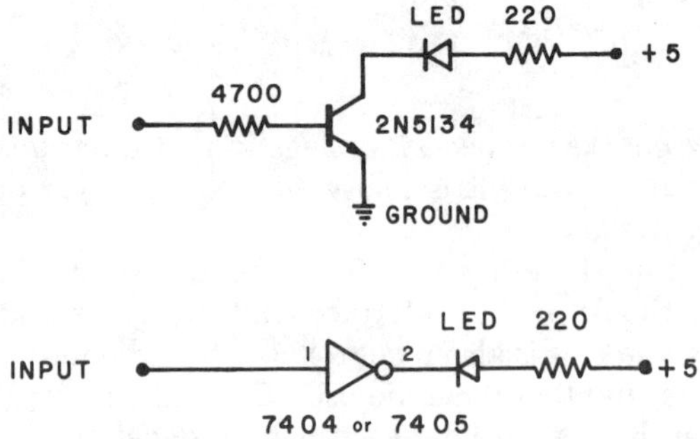


**Fig. A-1. Schematics of two simple lamp-monitor circuits that may be used in experiments.**

use of red LEDs is recommended, since they are inexpensive and readily seen. You will require at least eight of the individual lamp monitors to do the experiments in this book.

## LOGIC SWITCHES

Logic switches are simply switches that have been configured to provide either the logic one or the logic zero voltages to the TTL-compatible integrated circuits used in the experiments. A typical logic switch is shown in Fig. A-2. A single-pole, single-throw toggle switch or slide switch may be used. At least eight of the logic-switch circuits will be required in the experiments.

Fig. A-2. Schematic of simple logic-switch circuit that may be used to generate logic one or logic zero output.

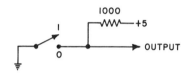

## PULSERS

The pulser circuit is used in the experiments to provide "clean" outputs that are free of the "bounce" that is normally associated with mechanical switches. Since most switches use spring-like metal contacts, the contacts will often open and close several times after the switch has been opened or closed. If such a mechanical switch is used to provide pulses to a counter, up to 30 to 40 pulses may be counted, depending on the type of switch used. Since there are many cases in which a clean logic one to logic zero, or logic zero to logic one, transition is required, a debounced switch is frequently useful. Mechanical switches are easily debounced, if they have contacts of the single-pole, double-throw form. A typical debouncing circuit is shown in Fig. A-3. In this case, two NAND gates have been used to form a flip-flop that may be set, or reset, by the switch. As shown in

Fig. A-3. Schematic for debounced pulser in which "cross-coupled" NAND gate has been used to eliminate contact bounce.

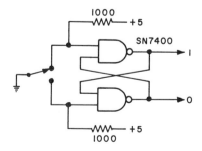

Fig. A-3, two outputs are available. With the switch in the position shown, the normal logic states are shown at the outputs of the two gates. When the switch is moved to the other position, the outputs of the NAND gates will switch. It is suggested that a momentary switch be used in the pulser circuits.

Lamp monitors, logic switches, and pulsers are all useful devices when breadboarding logic circuits. While the circuits shown in Figs. A-1 through A-3 are simple, you may not wish to build them yourself. Several companies produce digital breadboarding devices that incorporate lamp monitors, logic switches, and pulsers, as well as other digital functions. We suggest that you write to the following companies for information about their digital-electronic breadboarding systems:

E & L Instruments, Inc.
61 First Street
Derby, CT 06418

AP Products, Inc.
Mentor, OH 44060

PACCOM
14825 NE 40th, Suite 340
Redmond,WA 98025

# Parts Required for the Experiments

4 SN7402 Quad NOR-gate integrated circuit (IC)
2 SN7474 dual D-type flip-flop IC
2 DM8095 or SN74365 three-state input buffer (2@ per input port)
2 SN7475 Quad latch IC
1 NE5018 eight-bit D/A converter IC (Signetics Corporation)
1 SN7404 hex inverter IC
2 SN74LS373 three-state octal latch IC
1 0.01-$\mu$F, disc ceramic capacitor
1 4700-ohm, ¼-watt resistor
6 220-ohm, ¼-watt resistors
6 Visible LEDs (2@ red, 2@ green, and 2@ yellow)
1 10K, potentiometer trimmer-type
1 10K, ¼-watt resistor
1 100-$\mu$F electrolytic capacitor 16 WVDC
1 33K, ¼-watt resistor
1 150-pF disc capacitor
1 2200-ohm, ¼-watt resistor
1 ADC0804 analog-to-digital converter (National Semiconductor Corp.)
1 LM335 temperature sensor
4 1000-ohm, ¼-watt resistors

Besides the parts listed, you will need an assortment of SN7400, SN7408, SN7402, SN7410, SN7486, SN7430, and SN7493 integrated circuits for use in the logic-tester program in Experiment No. 14. We suggest that you read through this experiment to determine exactly what circuits you will want to test.

Other useful equipment: a ±12-volt power supply (for use with the D/A converter circuit), hook-up wire, an extra solderless breadboard, pulsers, logic switches, lamp monitors, and a voltmeter or vom.

Information about the analog converters is available from:

| | |
|---|---|
| ADC0804 A/D Converter | NE5018 D/A Converter |
| National Semiconductor Corp. | Signetics Corporation |
| 2900 Semiconductor Drive | 811 East Arques Avenue |
| Santa Clara, CA 95051 | Sunnyvale, CA 94086 |

Integrated circuits and components are available from many manufacturers, and we suggest that you check the many advertisements in the last pages of *Radio-Electronics, Popular Electronics, Kilobaud Microcomputing*, and other electronic magazines. We have tried to use standard parts wherever possible.

APPENDIX **C**

# 6502 Microprocessor
# Technical Data

The following pages contain some technical information pertaining to the 6502 microprocessor chip. This information has been abstracted from the *1980 Component Data Catalog,* from MOS Technology, Inc., 950 Rittenhouse Rd., Norristown, PA 19403. For more complete information about the 6502 processor and its associated family of functions, we suggest that you write to the manufacturer for a complete data sheet.

The 6502 chip is also available from:

Rockwell International                Synertek, Inc.
3310 Miraloma Avenue                3001 Stender Way
Anaheim, CA 92803                    Santa Clara, CA 95051

These manufacturers can also provide you with information about their 6502 microprocessor chip, and related devices.

# MCS6500 Microprocessors

- Single +5V Supply
- N-Channel, Silicon-Gate, Depletion-Load Technology
- 8-Bit Parallel Processing
- 56 Instructions
- Decimal and Binary Arithmetic

- 13 Addressing Modes
- Programmable Stack Pointer and Variable-Length Stack
- Usable With Any Type or Speed Memory
- 1 or 2 MHz Operation
- Pipelined Architecture

## DESCRIPTION

The MCS6500 Series microprocessors represent the first totally software-compatible microprocessor family. This family of products includes a range of software-compatible microprocessors which provide a selection of addressable memory range, interrupt input options and on-chip clock oscillators and drivers. All of the microprocessors in the MCS6500 group are software-compatible within the group and are bus compatible with the M6800 product offering.

The family includes five microprocessors with on-board clock oscillators and drivers and four microprocessors driven by external clocks. The on-chip clock versions are aimed at high-performance, low-cost applications where single-phase inputs, crystal or RC inputs provide the time base. The external clock versions are geared for multi-processor system applications where maximum timing control is mandatory. All versions of the microprocessors are available in 1 MHz and 2 MHz ("A" suffix on product numbers) maximum operating frequencies.

## MEMBERS OF THE FAMILY

| Part Numbers | | | | | | | |
|---|---|---|---|---|---|---|---|
| Plastic | Ceramic | Clocks | Pins | IRQ | NMI | RDY | Addressing |
| MCS6502 | MCS6502 | On-Chip | 40 | √ | √ | √ | 16 (64 K) |
| MCS6503 | MCS6503 | " | 28 | √ | √ | | 12 (4 K) |
| MCS6504 | MCS6504 | " | 28 | √ | | | 13 (8 K) |
| MCS6505 | MCS6505 | " | 28 | √ | | √ | 12 (4 K) |
| MCS6506 | MCS6506 | " | 28 | √ | | | 12 (4 K) |
| MCS6507 | MCS6507 | " | 28 | | | √ | 13 (8 K) |
| MCS6512 | MCS6512 | External | 40 | √ | √ | √ | 16 (64 K) |
| MCS6513 | MCS6513 | " | 28 | √ | √ | | 12 (4 K) |
| MCS6514 | MCS6514 | " | 28 | √ | | | 13 (8 K) |
| MCS6515 | MCS6515 | " | 28 | √ | | √ | 12 (4 K) |

## PIN FUNCTIONS

### Clocks (Φ1 and Φ2)

The MCS651X requires a two-phase, non-overlapping clock that runs at the $V_{CC}$ voltage level.

The MCS650X clocks are supplied with an internal clock generator. The frequency of these clocks is externally controlled. Details of this feature are discussed in the MCS6502 portion of this data sheet.

### Address Bus (A0-A15)

(See sections on each processor for respective address lines on those devices.)

These outputs are TTL-compatible, capable of driving one standard TTL load and 130pF.

### Data Bus (D0-D7)

Eight pins are used for the data bus. This is a bi-directional bus, transferring data to and from the device and peripherals. The outputs are three-state buffers capable of driving one standard TTL load and 130pF.

### Data Bus Enable (DBE)

This TTL-compatible input allows external control of the three-state data output buffers and will enable the microprocessor bus driver when in the high state. In normal operation, DBE would be driven by the phase two (Φ2) clock, thus allowing data input from microprocessor only during Φ2. During the read cycle, the data bus drivers are internally disabled, becoming essentially an open circuit. To disable data bus drivers externally, DBE should be held low.

### Ready (RDY)

This input signal allows the user to single-cycle the microprocessor on all cycles except write cycles. A negative transition to the low state during or coincident with phase one (Φ1) will halt the microprocessor with the output address lines reflecting the current address being fetched. This condition will remain through a subsequent phase two (Φ2) in which the Ready signal is low. This feature allows microprocessor interfacing with low-speed PROMS as well as fast (max. 2 cycle) Direct Memory Access (DMA). If Ready is low during a write cycle, it is ignored until the following read operation.

### Interrupt Request (IRQ)

This TTL-compatible signal requests that an interrupt sequence begin within the microprocessor. The microprocessor will complete the current instruction being executed before recognizing the request. At that time, the interrupt mask bit in the Status Code Register will be examined. If the interrupt mask flag is not set, the microprocessor will begin an interrupt sequence. The Program Counter and Processor Status Register are stored in the stack. The microprocessor will then set the interrupt mask flag high so that no further interrupts may occur. At the end of this cycle, the program counter low will be loaded from address FFFE, and program counter high from location FFFF, transferring program control to the memory vector located at these addresses. The RDY signal must be in the high state for any interrupt to be recognized. A 3KΩ external resistor should be used for proper wire-OR operation.

### Non-Maskable Interrupt (NMI)

A negative-going edge on this input requests that a non-maskable interrupt sequence be generated within the microprocessor.

NMI is an unconditional interrupt. Following completion of the current instruction, the sequence of operations defined for IRQ will be performed, regardless of the state of the interrupt mask flag. The vector address loaded into the program counter, low and high, are locations FFFA and FFFB respectively, transferring program control to the memory vector located at these addresses. The instructions loaded at these locations cause the microprocessor to branch to a non-maskable interrupt routine in memory.

NMI also requires an external 3KΩ register to $V_{CC}$ for proper wire-OR operations.

Inputs IRQ and NMI are hardware interrupts lines that are sampled during Φ2 and will begin the appropriate interrupt routine on the Φ1 following the completion of the current instruction.

### Set Overflow Flag (S.O.)

A NEGATIVE-going edge on this input sets the overflow bit in the Status Code Register. This signal is sampled on the trailing edge of Φ1.

### SYNC

This output line is provided to identify those cycles during which the microprocessor is doing an OP CODE fetch. The SYNC line goes high during Φ1 of an OP CODE fetch and stays high for the remainder of that cycle. If the RDY line is pulled low during the Φ1 clock pulse in which SYNC went high, the processor will stop in its current state and will remain in the state until the RDY line goes high. In this manner, the SYNC signal can be used to control RDY to cause single instruction execution.

### Reset

This input is used to reset or start the microprocessor from a power down condition. During the time that this line is held low, writing to or from the microprocessor is inhibited. When a positive edge is detected on the input, the microprocessor will immediately begin the reset sequence.

After a system initialization time of six clock cycles, the mask interrupt flag will be set and the microprocessor will load the program counter from memory vector locations FFFC and FFFD. This is the start location for program control.

After $V_{CC}$ reaches 4.75 volts in a power up routine, reset must be held low for at least two clock cycles. At this time the R/W and (SYNC) signal will become valid.

When the reset signal goes high following these two clock cycles, the microprocessor will proceed with the normal reset procedure detailed above.

**INTERNAL ARCHITECTURE**

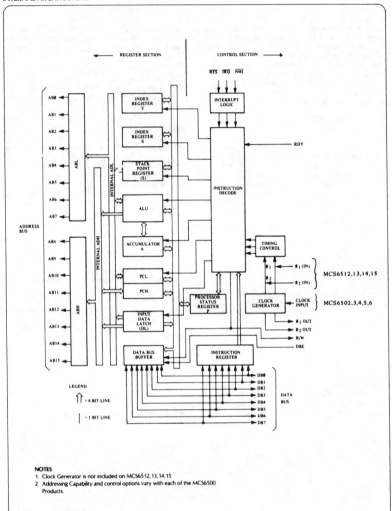

NOTES
1. Clock Generator is not included on MCS6512,13,14,15
2. Addressing Capability and control options vary with each of the MCS6500
   Products.

## INSTRUCTION SET—ALPHABETICAL SEQUENCE

ADC  Add Memory to Accumulator with Carry
AND  "AND" Memory with Accumulator
ASL  Shift left One Bit (Memory or Accumulator)

BCC  Branch on Carry Clear
BCS  Branch on Carry Set
BEQ  Branch on Result Zero
BIT  Test Bits in Memory with Accumulator
BMI  Branch on Result Minus
BNE  Branch on Result not Zero
BPL  Branch on Result Plus
BRK  Force Break
BVC  Branch on Overflow Clear
BVS  Branch on Overflow Set

CLC  Clear Carry Flag
CLD  Clear Decimal Mode
CLI  Clear Interrupt Disable Bit
CLV  Clear Overflow Flag
CMP  Compare Memory and Accumulator
CPX  Compare Memory and Index X
CPY  Compare Memory and Index Y

DEC  Decrement Memory by One
DEX  Decrement Index X by One
DEY  Decrement Index Y by One

EOR  "Exclusive-or" Memory with Accumulator

INC  Increment Memory by One
INX  Increment Index by One
INY  Increment Index Y by One

JMP  Jump to New Location
JSR  Jump to New Location Saving Return Address

LDA  Load Accumulator with Memory
LDX  Load Index X with Memory
LDY  Load Index Y with Memory
LSR  Shift One Bit Right (Memory or Accumulator)

NOP  No Operation

ORA  "OR" Memory with Accumulator

PHA  Push Accumulator on Stack
PHP  Push Processor Status on Stack

PLA  Pull Accumulator from Stack
PLP  Pull Processor Status from Stack

ROL  Rotate One Bit Left (Memory or Accumulator)
ROR  Rotate One Bit Right (Memory or Accumulator)
RTI  Return from Interrupt
RTS  Return from Subroutine

SBC  Subtract Memory from Accumulator with Borrow
SEC  Set Carry Flag
SED  Set Decimal Mode
SEI  Set Interrupt Disable Status
STA  Store Accumulator in Memory
STX  Store Index X in Memory
STY  Store Index Y in Memory

TAX  Transfer Accumulator to Index X
TAY  Transfer Accumulator to Index Y
TSX  Transfer Stack Pointer to Index X
TXA  Transfer Index X to Accumulator
TXS  Transfer Index X to Stack Pointer
TYA  Transfer Index Y to Accumulator

## ADDRESSING MODES

**Accumulator Addressing.** This form of addressing is represented with a one-byte instruction, implying an operation on the accumulator.

**Immediate Addressing.** In immediate addressing, the operand is contained in the second byte of the instruction, with no further memory addressing required.

**Absolute Addressing.** In absolute addressing, the second byte of the instruction specifies the eight low-order bits of the effective address while the third byte specifies the eight high-order bits. Thus, the absolute addressing mode allows access to the entire 65K bytes of addressable memory.

**Zero Page Addressing.** The zero page instructions allow for shorter code and execution times by only fetching the second byte of the instruction and assuming a zero high-address byte. Careful use of the zero page can result in significant increase in code efficiency.

**Indexed Zero Page Addressing.** (X, Y indexing) — This form of addressing is used in conjunction with the index register and is referred to as "Zero Page, X" or "Zero Page, Y". The effective address is calculated by adding the second byte to the contents of the index register. Since this is a form of "Zero Page" addressing, the content of the second byte references a location in page zero. Additionally due to the "Zero Page" addressing nature of this mode, no carry is added to the high order 8 bits of memory and crossing of page boundaries does not occur.

**Indexed Absolute Addressing.** (X, Y indexing) — This form of addressing is used in conjunction with X and Y index register and is referred to as "Absolute, X", and "Absolute, Y". The effective address is formed by adding the contents of X or Y to the address contained in the second and third bytes of the instruction. This mode allows the index register to contain the index or count value and the instruction to contain the base address. This type of indexing allows any location referencing and the index to modify multiple fields resulting in reduced coding and execution time.

**Implied Addressing.** In the implied addressing mode, the address containing the operand is implicitly stated in the operation code of the instruction.

**Relative Addressing.** Relative addressing is used only with branch instructions and establishes a destination for the conditional branch. The second byte of the instruction becomes the operand which is an offset added to the contents of the lower eight bits of the program counter when the counter is set at the next instruction. The range of the offset is −128 to +127 bytes from the next instruction.

**Indexed Indirect Addressing.** In indexed indirect addressing (referred to as Indirect, X), the second byte of the instruction is added to the contents of the X index register, discarding the carry. The result of this addition points to a memory location on page zero whose contents is the low-order eight bits of the effective address. The next memory location in page zero contains the high-order eight bits of the effective address. Both memory locations specifying the high and low-order bytes of the effective address must be in page zero.

**Indirect Indexed Addressing.** In indirect indexed addressing (referred to as Indirect, Y), the second byte of the instruction points to a memory location in page zero. The contents on this memory location is added to the contents of the Y index register, the result being the low-order eight bits of the effective address. The carry from this addition is added to the contents of the next page zero memory location, the result being the high-order eight bits of the effective address.

**Absolute Indirect.** The second byte of the instruction contains the low-order eight bits of a memory location. The high-order eight bits of that memory location is contained in the third byte of the instruction. The contents of the fully specified memory location is the low-order byte of the effective address. The next memory location contains the high-order byte of the effective address which is loaded into the 16-bit program counter.

## ABSOLUTE MAXIMUM RATINGS

| Rating | Symbol | Value | Unit |
|---|---|---|---|
| Supply Voltage | $V_{CC}$ | −0.3 to +7.0 | Vdc |
| Input Voltage | $V_{IN}$ | −0.3 to +7.0 | Vdc |
| Operating Temperature | $T_A$ | 0 to +70 | °C |
| Storage Temperature | $T_{STG}$ | −55 to +150 | °C |

## CAUTION
*This device contains input protection against damage due to high static voltages or electric fields; however, precautions should be taken to avoid application of voltages higher than the maximum rating.*

## CLOCK TIMING—MCS6512, 13, 14, 15

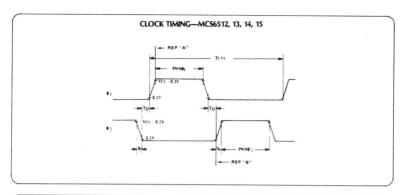

## TIMING FOR READING DATA FROM MEMORY OR PERIPHERALS

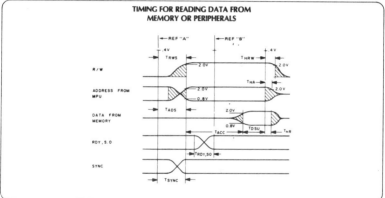

## TIMING FOR WRITING DATA TO MEMORY OR PERIPHERALS

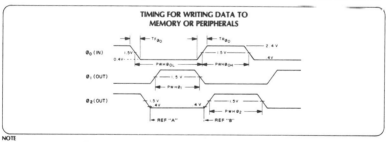

NOTE
"REF." means Reference Points on clocks.

**ELECTRICAL CHARACTERISTICS**  ($V_{CC}$ = 5.0V ± 5%, $V_{SS}$ = 0, $T_A$ = 25°C)

$\emptyset_1$, $\emptyset_2$ applies to MCS6512, 13, 14, 15, $\emptyset_{o\ (in)}$ applies to MCS6502, 03, 04, 05 and 06

| Symbol | Parameter | Min | Typ | Max | Unit | Test Condition |
|---|---|---|---|---|---|---|
| $V_{IH}$ | Input High Voltage | $V_{SS}$ + 2.4<br>$V_{CC}$ − 0.2 | | $V_{CC}$<br>$V_{CC}$ + 0.25 | Vdc | Logic, $\emptyset_{o\ (in)}$<br>$\emptyset_1$, $\emptyset_2$ |
| $V_{IL}$ | Input Low Voltage | $V_{SS}$ − 0.3<br>$V_{SS}$ − 0.3 | | $V_{SS}$ + 0.4<br>$V_{SS}$ + 0.2 | Vdc | Logic, $\emptyset_{o\ (in)}$<br>$\emptyset_1$, $\emptyset_2$ |
| $V_{IHT}$ | Input High Threshold Voltage | $V_{SS}$ + 2.0 | | | Vdc | $\overline{RES}$, $\overline{NMI}$, RDY, $\overline{IRQ}$, Data, S.O. |
| $V_{ILT}$ | Input Low Threshold Voltage | | | $V_{SS}$ + 0.8 | Vdc | $\overline{RES}$, $\overline{NMI}$, RDY, $\overline{IRQ}$, Data, S.O. |
| $I_{IN}$ | Input Leakage Current | | | 2.5<br>100<br>10.0 | μA<br>μA<br>μA | ($V_{IN}$ = 0 to 5.25V, $V_{CC}$ = 0)<br>Logic (Excl. RDY, S.O.)<br>$\emptyset_1$, $\emptyset_2$<br>$\emptyset_{o\ (in)}$ |
| $I_{TSI}$ | Three-State (Off State) Input Current | | | 10 | μA | ($V_{IN}$ = 0.4 to 2.4V, $V_{CC}$ = 5.25V)<br>Data Lines |
| $V_{OH}$ | Output High Voltage | $V_{SS}$ + 2.4 | | | Vdc | ($I_{LOAD}$ = − 100μAdc, $V_{CC}$ = 4.75V)<br>SYNC, Data, A0–A15, R/W |
| $V_{OL}$ | Output Low Voltage | | | $V_{SS}$ + 0.4 | Vdc | ($I_{LOAD}$ = 1.6mAdc, $V_{CC}$ = 4.75V)<br>SYNC, Data, A0–A15, R/W |
| $P_D$ | Power Dissipation | | .25 | .70 | W | |
| C<br>$C_{IN}$<br><br>$C_{OUT}$<br>$C_{\emptyset_{o\ (in)}}$<br>$C_{\emptyset_1}$<br>$C_{\emptyset_2}$ | Capacitance | | <br><br><br><br>30<br>50 | <br>10<br>15<br>12<br>50<br>50<br>80 | pF | ($V_{IN}$ = 0, $T_A$ = 25°C, f = 1MHz)<br>Logic<br>Data<br>A0–A15, R/W, SYNC<br>$\emptyset_{o\ (in)}$<br>$\emptyset_1$<br>$\emptyset_2$ |

**NOTE**
$\overline{IRQ}$ and $\overline{NMI}$ require 3K pull-up resistors.

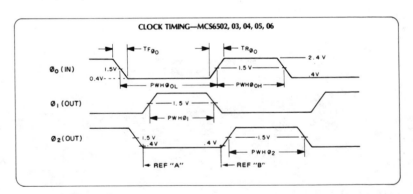

CLOCK TIMING—MCS6502, 03, 04, 05, 06

## MCS6500

**1 MHz TIMING**

**CLOCK TIMING—MCS6512, 13, 14, 15**

| Symbol | Characteristic | | Min | Typ | Max | Unit |
|---|---|---|---|---|---|---|
| $T_{CYC}$ | Cycle Time | | 1000 | | | nsec |
| PWH $\phi$1<br>PWH $\phi$2 | Clock Pulse Width<br>(Measured at $V_{CC} - 0.2$ V) | $\phi$1<br>$\phi$2 | 430<br>470 | | | nsec |
| $T_F$ | Fall Time (Measured from 0.2 V to $V_{CC} - 0.2$ V) | | | | 25 | nsec |
| $T_D$ | Delay Time Between Clocks (Measured at 0.2 V) | | 0 | | | nsec |

**CLOCK TIMING—MCS6502, 03, 04, 05, 06**

| Symbol | Characteristic | Min | Typ | Max | Unit |
|---|---|---|---|---|---|
| $T_{CYC}$ | Cycle Time | 1000 | | | ns |
| PWH$\phi_0$ | $\phi_{0\,(IN)}$ Pulse Width (measured at 1.5 V) | 460 | | 520 | ns |
| TR$\phi_0$, TF$\phi_0$ | $\phi_{0\,(IN)}$ Rise, Fall Time | | | 10 | ns |
| $T_D$ | Delay Time Between Clocks (measured at 1.5 V) | 5 | | | ns |
| PWH$\phi_1$ | $\phi_{1\,(OUT)}$ Pulse Width (measured at 1.5 V) | PWH$\phi_{oL}-20$ | | PWH$\phi_{oL}$ | ns |
| PWH$\phi_2$ | $\phi_{1\,(OUT)}$ Pulse Width (measured at 1.5 V) | PWH$\phi_{oH}-40$ | | PWH$\phi_{oH}-10$ | ns |
| $T_R$, $T_F$ | $\phi_{1\,(OUT)}$, $\phi_{2\,(OUT)}$ Rise, Fall Time<br>(measured .8 V to 2.0 V)<br>(Load = 30pF + 1 TTL) | | | 25 | ns |

**READ/WRITE TIMING**

| Symbol | Characteristic | Min | Typ | Max | Unit |
|---|---|---|---|---|---|
| $T_{RWS}$ | Read/Write Setup Time From MCS6500 | | 100 | 300 | ns |
| $T_{ADS}$ | Address Setup Time From MCS6500 | | 100 | 300 | ns |
| $T_{ACC}$ | Memory Read Access Time | | | 575 | ns |
| $T_{DSU}$ | Data Stability Time Period | 100 | | | ns |
| $T_{HR}$ | Data Hold Time – Read | 10 | | | ns |
| $T_{HW}$ | Data Hold Time – Write | 30 | 60 | | ns |
| $T_{MDS}$ | Data Setup Time From MCS6500 | | 150 | 200 | ns |
| $T_{RDY}$ | RDY, S.O. Setup Time | 100 | | | ns |
| $T_{SYNC}$ | SYNC Setup Time From MCS6500 | | | 350 | ns |
| $T_{HA}$ | Address Hold Time | 30 | 60 | | ns |
| $T_{HRW}$ | R/W Hold Time | 30 | 60 | | ns |

## 2 MHz TIMING

### CLOCK TIMING—MCS6512, 13, 14, 15, 16

| Symbol | Characteristic | | Min | Typ | Max | Unit |
|---|---|---|---|---|---|---|
| $T_{CYC}$ | Cycle Time | | 500 | | | nsec |
| PWH $\phi1$<br>PWH $\phi2$ | Clock Pulse Width<br>(Measured at $V_{CC}$ − 0.2 V) | $\phi1$<br>$\phi2$ | 215<br>235 | | | nsec |
| $T_F$ | Fall Time (Measured from 0.2 V to $V_{CC}$ − 0.2 V) | | | | 12 | nsec |
| $T_D$ | Delay Time Between Clocks (Measured at 0.2 V) | | 0 | | | nsec |

### CLOCK TIMING—MCS6502, 03, 04, 05, 06

| Symbol | Characteristic | Min | Typ | Max | Unit |
|---|---|---|---|---|---|
| $T_{CYC}$ | Cycle Time | 500 | | | ns |
| $PWH\phi_o$ | $\phi_{o\ (IN)}$ Pulse Width (measured at 1.5 V) | 240 | | 260 | ns |
| $TR\phi_o$, $TF\phi_o$ | $\phi_{o\ (IN)}$ Rise, Fall Time | | | 10 | ns |
| $T_D$ | Delay Time Between Clocks (measured at 1.5 V) | 5 | | | ns |
| $PWH\phi_1$ | $\phi_{1\ (OUT)}$ Pulse Width (measured at 1.5 V) | $PWH\phi_{oL}-20$ | | $PWH\phi_{oL}$ | ns |
| $PWH\phi_2$ | $\phi_{2\ (OUT)}$ Pulse Width (measured at 1.5 V) | $PWH\phi_{oH}-40$ | | $PWH\phi_{oH}-10$ | ns |
| $T_R$, $T_F$ | $\phi_{1\ (OUT)}$, $\phi_{2\ (OUT)}$ Rise, Fall Time<br>(measured .8 V to 2.0 V)<br>(Load = 30pF + 1 TTL) | | | 25 | ns |

### READ/WRITE TIMING

| Symbol | Characteristic | Min | Typ | Max | Unit |
|---|---|---|---|---|---|
| $T_{RWS}$ | Read/Write Setup Time From MCS6500A | | 100 | 150 | ns |
| $T_{ADS}$ | Address Setup Time From MCS6500A | | 100 | 150 | ns |
| $T_{ACC}$ | Memory Read Access Time | | | 300 | ns |
| $T_{DSU}$ | Data Stability Time Period | 50 | | | ns |
| $T_{HR}$ | Data Hold Time − Read | 10 | | | ns |
| $T_{HW}$ | Data Hold Time − Write | 30 | 60 | | ns |
| $T_{MDS}$ | Data Setup Time From MCS6500A | | 75 | 100 | ns |
| $T_{RDY}$ | RDY, S.O. Setup Time | 50 | | | ns |
| $T_{SYNC}$ | SYNC Setup Time From MCS6500A | | | 175 | ns |
| $T_{HA}$ | Address Hold Time | 30 | 60 | | ns |
| $T_{HRW}$ | R/W Hold Time | 30 | 60 | | ns |

APPENDIX **D**

# Apple Interface
# Breadboard Parts

Parts required for the construction of the Apple Interface Breadboard:

| | |
|---|---|
| IC 1 & 7 | 16-pin resistor network, eight independent 1000-ohm resistors |
| IC 2 & 6 | 8-position DIP switch (on-off) |
| IC 3,4, & 5 | SN74LS85 Quad comparator IC (*Do Not Substitute* SN74L85) |
| IC 8 | SN74LS20 dual four-input NAND gate IC |
| IC 9 | SN74365 or DM8095 three-state buffer |
| IC 10 & 11 | 8216 noninverting bus buffer, Intel or equivalent |
| IC 12 | SN74154 decoder IC |
| IC 13 | SN7404 inverter IC |
| IC 14 | SN74123 or SN74SL123 dual monostable IC |
| IC 15 | LM319N dual comparator (14-pin package) |
| IC 16, 17, 18, & 20 | High-quality 16-pin IC sockets, Augat 516-AG-10D, or equivalent |
| IC 19 | High-quality 8-pin IC socket, Augat 508-AG-10D, or equivalent |
| D1 - D4 | 1N4001 50 piv, 1-ampere diodes* |
| D5 | Yellow LED |
| D6 | Red LED |
| D7 | Green LED |
| D8 & D9 | 1N4148 or 1N4154, small-signal diodes |

| | |
|---|---|
| R1 & R8 | 1000-ohm, ¼-watt resistor |
| R2 & R3 | 220-ohm, ¼-watt resistor |
| R4 & R5 | 47K, ¼-watt resistor |
| R6 | 3900-ohm, ¼-watt resistor |
| R7 | 2200-ohm, ¼-watt resistor |
| C1 | 2200-$\mu$F, 16 V dcw electrolytic capacitor (axial)* |
| C2, 4 & 5 | 0.1-$\mu$F disc ceramic, 50-volt capacitors |
| C3 & C6 | 1-$\mu$F, 35 V dcw tantalum electrolytic capacitors |
| C7 & C8 | 3.3 $\mu$F, 50 V dcw electrolytic capacitors (axial) |
| VR | LM309K 5-volt, 1-amp voltage regulator* |
| P1 | Molex right-angle 6-pin connector (PN 09-75-1061) optional |
| | Requires 1@ mating female housing (PN09-50-7061) and 6@ connector pins (PN 08-50-0106 or 08-50-0108) |
| P2 | 40-pin right-angle jumper header, AP Products 923875R, or equivalent |
| T1 | 12.6 V ac transformer 1 amp |
| Misc. | 11 16-pin IC sockets |
| | 3 14-pin IC sockets |
| | 1 24-pin IC socket |
| | Cable assembly: 40-pin header on one end, with a 40-pin card edge connector on the other, facing the same direction |
| | Solderless breadboard socket, SK-10, Superstrip, or equivalent, 4@ 4-40 × ⅝ flat-head mach. screws, 4@ #4 internal-tooth lock washers, 4@ #4 hex nuts. |
| | Heat sink for VR, 2@ 4-40 × ½ mach. screws, 2@ #4 internal-tooth lockwashers, 2@ #4 hex nuts, mica insulator, thermal grease (optional). |
| | Power cord |

The parts marked with "*" are not required if an external +5-volt power supply will be used to power the system.

A complete package, containing a case power supply, etc., is available from

E & L Instruments, Inc.
61 First Street
Derby, CT 06418

# Printed-Circuit
# Board Artwork

This appendix contains artwork that may be used to make a printed-circuit board of the Apple interfacing breadboard. Since the artwork has been reduced, it must be enlarged before it can be used. We recommend that you have a print shop make a high-contrast film negative, or positive, depending on the process that you will use. The long thick black line in each of the three diagrams should be enlarged so that it is four (4) inches long. The process-camera operator should be able to correct the enlarging process so that the resulting film is the right size for the printed-circuit board. You may not choose to use the parts overlay, but it has been provided as a guide to the placement of the various parts.

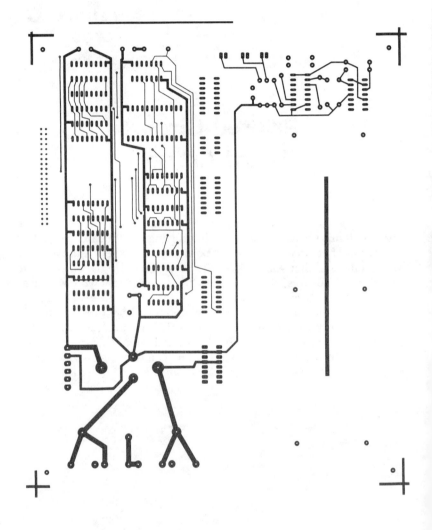

Fig. E-1. Printed-circuit board artwork for component side of interface breadboard (right reading).

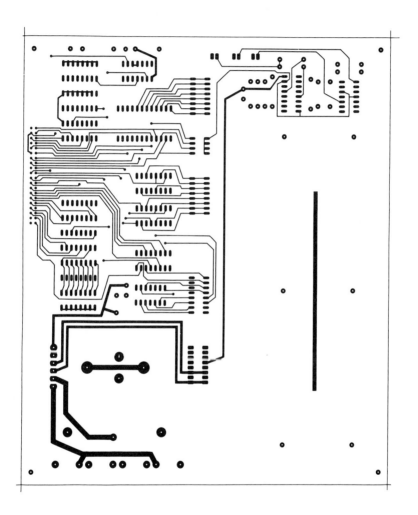

Fig. E-2. Printed-circuit board artwork for solder side of interface breadboard (reverse reading).

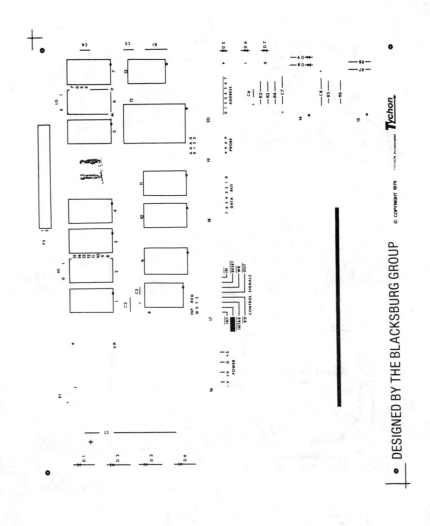

Fig. E-3. Nomenclature overlay for interface breadboard (right reading).

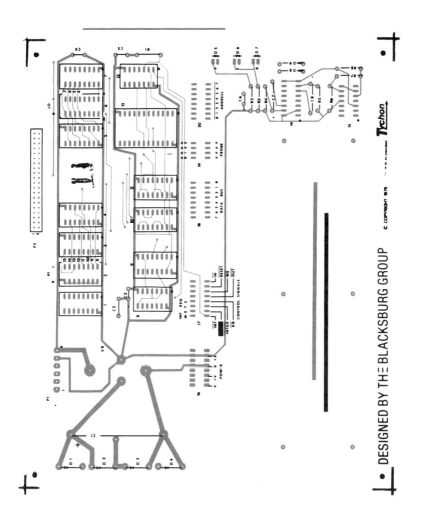

Fig. E-4. Component nomenclature overlay superimposed on component-side foil
pattern, may be used as parts placement guide.

# Index

# READER SERVICE CARD

   To better serve you, the reader, please take a moment to fill out this card, or a copy of it, for us. Not only will you be kept up to date on the Blacksburg Series books, but as an extra bonus, **we will randomly select five cards every month, from all of the cards sent to us during the previous month. The names that are drawn will win, absolutely free, a book from the Blacksburg Continuing Education Series.** Therefore, make sure to indicate your choice in the space provided below. For a complete listing of all the books to choose from, refer to the inside front cover of this book. Please, one card per person. Give everyone a chance.

   In order to find out who has won a book in your area, call (703) 953-1861 anytime during the night or weekend. When you do call, an answering machine will let you know the monthly winners. Too good to be true? Just give us a call.  Good luck.

If I win, please send me a copy of:

_____

I understand that this book will be sent to me absolutely free, if my card is selected.

   For our information, how about telling us a little about yourself. We are interested in your occupation, how and where you normally purchase books and the books that you would like to see in the Blacksburg Series. We are also interested in finding authors for the series, so if you have a book idea, write to The Blacksburg Group, Inc., P.O. Box 242, Blacksburg, VA 24060 and ask for an Author Packet. We are also interested in TRS-80, APPLE, OSI and PET BASIC programs.

My occupation is _____

I buy books through/from _____

Would you buy books through the mail? _____

I'd like to see a book about _____

Name _____

Address _____

City _____

State _____ Zip _____

MAIL TO: BOOKS, BOX 715, BLACKSBURG, VA  24060
!!!!!PLEASE PRINT!!!!!